AVAILABLE TITLES

Build Your Own Table

Copyright © 2023 by Dr. Y. Bur. All rights reserved.

Visit www.RoarPublishingGroup.com for more information. No part of this publication may be reproduced, stored in a retrieval system, or transmitted in any way by any means, electronic, mechanical, photocopy, recording, or otherwise, without the prior permission of the author except as provided by USA copyright law.

Book design copyright © 2023 by R.O.A.R. International Group. All rights reserved.

R.O.A.R. Publishing Group
581 N. Park Ave. Ste. #725
Apopka, FL 32704
ROAR-58-2316
762-758-2316
www.RoarPublishingGroup.com
DrYBur@gmail.com

Published in the United States of America
ISBN: 978-1-948936-76-7
$22.88

Table of Contents

Introduction 9
Building Block 1 13
   Blueprinted Building Blocks 13
Building Block 2 17
   Love and Compassion 17
Building Block 3 23
   Attraction 23
Building Block 4 29
   Seedtime and Harvest 29
Building Block 5 33
   Forgiveness 33
Building Block 6 37
   Abundance 37
Building Block 7 41
   Detachment 41
Building Block 8 47

Intention	47
Building Block 9	53
Unity	53
Building Block 10	57
Balance	57
Building Block 11	61
Surrender	61
Building Block 12	69
Reflection	69
Building Block 13	73
Cause and Effect	73
Building Block 14	77
Non-judgment	77
Building Block 15	81
Manifestation	81
Building Block 16	89
Transcendence	89
Building Block 17	93
Self-Love	93
Building Block 18	101

Responsibility 101
Building Block 19 109
Resonance 109
Building Block 20 117
Service 117
Building Block 21 127
Transformation 127
Building Block 22 133
Purpose 133
Divine Status 141
Reciprocity 144
Self-Discipline 149
Self-Improvement 151

INTRODUCTION

Have you sat at someone's table who did not want you there? Have you experienced not being invited to the table where you provided the meal? Have you been excluded from the table because you do not fit in with the crowd? Then again, have you been excluded from the table because no one wants to hear your viewpoint? Do they think you are unhinged or pulling for straws for being who you are? Are you excluded from the table because everyone will know that it is your recipe being served? Have you only been invited to the table to be led to the slaughter, humiliated, or pounced on? Or, are you the best-kept secret?

In *Building Your Own Table*, the vital questions must be asked to ensure the table actually belongs to you. If it does not, it is time to create your own with the recipes, stories, and delights hidden in your Divine Greatness with no shame attached.

Unbeknown to most, your recipes, stories, and delights are at your beck and call; however, you must learn how to build with Spiritual Building Blocks, *As It Pleases God*, leaving the plastic for the naysayers, onlookers, and jokesters. What does this mean? When you get your heart and mind right, *As It Pleases God*, all that should be on your table will follow, and no one can stop it besides you.

Finding the balance between our purpose, goals, dreams, and passions can be challenging, but knowing the difference can lead us toward a particular Spiritual Path, enabling them to coexist without confusion, shame, or dismay. Using the *Spiritual Building Blocks to Build Our Own Table* can change the trajectory of our lives by simply knowing the difference between our skills, talents, and gifts without settling for mediocrity.

Once we are in the know, *As It Pleases God*, we can better understand our strengths and weaknesses, causing our average skills, talents, and gifts to become an upgrade to Spiritual Skills, Talents, and Gifts, making our natural Supernatural. Is this humanly possible? Absolutely! We are Spiritual Beings having a human experience with a powerful combination of GREATNESS hidden within our loins. If we do not understand who we are and why we are, or dibble and dabble in negativity, we sucker-punch or turn on ourselves without knowing it. Then again, we may break tables instead of building them while feeling right or justified in our own eyes with the 'get them before they get me' mentality.

When *Building Our Own Table*, our *Spiritual Building Blocks* are essential life-giving elements that form the foundation of our substance, hope, and faith. All of these are unveiled in our principles, values, habits, and skills, shaping our character, guiding our actions, thoughts, and beliefs, and helping us grow, learn, and achieve.

Can we function without using *Spiritual Building Blocks?* Absolutely. We all have free will to do whatever, whenever, and however. Just remember, it takes the same amount of energy to use, avoid, or lose them. So, it behooves us to use the Spiritual Tools available to avoid turning on ourselves without knowing it.

Fighting against a Divine System designed to assist us is not wise. Why? It is designed to help us overcome challenges, combat trauma, cope with uncertainty, and face adversity with resilience and courage to enrich our lives. Those who say they do not want to enrich their lives only fool themselves because survival and adaptation are in our nature, Divinely Woven in our DNA. What does this mean? No one is exempt from the natural tendency to succeed; we only lack the know-how, how-to, or capital.

Once we have the know-how or how-to, we can grow great according to our Predestined Blueprint. What about capital? Once we are in Purpose on purpose, God will provide the provisions if we BELIEVE and Spiritually Till our own ground, *As It Pleases Him.* The goal is to unveil the Divine Blueprint from within first. Why? It is Spiritually Designed to finance itself, especially if it is God-Given and Heavenly Ordained. Our responsibility is to reflect our faith in God and our commitment to His Divine Will, developing, improving, regrafting, and refining ourselves with a work-in-progress mentality.

Why must we become a work-in-progress? When dealing with the Heavenly of Heavens, we must remain on a learning curve through much practice, reflection, testing, revamping, and feedback in or out of our Spiritual Classroom. If we become static in learning, we will become stiff-necked, disobedient, egotistical, and resistant to change, leading to all types of negative attachments, yokes, or disparities.

Building Our Own Table is not easy, quick, or an overnight process. Why? Spiritual Development, *As It Pleases God*, takes time, effort, and dedication, similar to the Seedtime and Harvest analogy. Although doing things in God's Divine Way is unpopular, it comes with a sense of fulfillment, joy, and peace that money cannot buy. Relying on God's Divine Grace, Power, and Presence is a sought-after state of being by all. Still, it is only used by a few, *As It Pleases Him*. What does this mean? We often do what pleases us without adding the Holy Trinity into our equational efforts with the Spiritual Principles needed to sustain our Divine Positioning in the Kingdom.

If we view our *Spiritual Building Blocks* as a Divine Gift from the Heavenly of Heavens, they will change our life's trajectory. Eminently, granting us the keys to unlock the doors of opportunities and endless possibilities, making our names GREAT, as we become the person God created us to be.

The time is now to *Build Your Own Table* of substance...so let us discuss one *Building Block* at a time to place a Spiritual Seal on *The WHY Blueprint* of your life. If you have not read *The WHY Blueprint*, it is best to do so before attempting to *Build Your Own Table*. What is the purpose of doing so? You must know your WHY; if not, you may figuratively find yourself hopping over dollars to pick up a nickel, calling good evil and evil good.

BUILDING BLOCK 1
Blueprinted Building Blocks

Spiritual Laws are a set of principles governing the universe and the way it works. These laws are not physical laws like gravity or thermodynamics, but they are Spiritual Guidelines that help us live our lives and align with our Divinely Blueprinted Purpose. Some of the most essential Spiritual Laws include the Law of Reciprocity, Seedtime and Harvest, Forgiveness, Abundance, and Cause and Effect. By understanding and applying these Spiritual Laws as our *Blueprinted Building Blocks*, we can create a more fulfilling and meaningful existence and ultimately achieve our highest and greatest potential.

With our *Blueprinted Building Blocks*, the goal is to obtain the capitalization where there was a lowercase. This analogy is similar to higher and lesser laws, as gravity is a lesser law that can be superseded by a higher one. What does this mean? Most would think gravity is the highest and most powerful law, but it is not. A higher law can overcome it, but we must know what it is, such as the Law of Aerodynamics,

Supernatural Miracles, Heavenly Divinity, or Divine Intervention.

In *Building Our Own Table*, we must know what Spiritual Blocks are and what they are not. Plus, we must know and understand which ones are required according to our Predestined Blueprint to ensure we become effective in our efforts, doing all things in the Spirit of Excellence. Why are we expected to operate in the Spirit of Excellence? Excellence does not mean perfect; it is simply doing and giving our best with good-willed intentions in the Spirit of Righteousness.

We are not often taught Spiritual Laws, *As It Pleases God*; as a result, we are left to our own devices, trying to figure things out or plugging and playing on our own terms. With our *Blueprinted Building Blocks*, we must become aware of them. Why? They are the TOOLS used to Spiritually Till our own ground. In addition, they can serve as measures to prune us from what does or does not rightfully belong to us, helping us get rid of the dry and dull people, places, and things stunting our growth or blocking our Divine Access.

Why is awareness of Spiritual Laws required? In the Eye of God, Spiritual Laws will serve as a BRICK or Building Block, eventually guiding us step-by-step on our Blueprinted Journey. What does this mean? Everyone's Blueprinted Journey is different, containing individualized sets of instructions; therefore, there is no formal set of cookie-cutter instructions. The bottom line is that we need the presence of the Holy Trinity involved in our day-to-day operations to download what is Divine.

If we focus on stepping without building a solid foundation from the inside out, we will fall short without knowing why, how, and where. Therefore, in *The WHY*

Blueprint, we reverse engineer the mindset to incorporate Spiritual Principles. What is the purpose of doing so? We are Spiritual Beings having a human experience, and our Divine Blueprint is engineered as such. If we approach our Predestined Blueprint as a know-it-all human, it will reject us. Why? As a know-it-all human, it tells our Guarded Blueprint that we know nothing about who we are as a Spiritual Being, so we are rejected and placed back into the cycle of déjà vu, Spiritual Classroom, or trauma queue. Really? Yes, really!

For example, there are laws governing owning a vehicle and the roads used to facilitate our driving privileges, right? The same applies to our Spiritual Gifts, Calling, Creativity, Wisdom, and Knowledge, especially when dealing with *The WHY Blueprint*. For this reason, it is my reasonable service to enlighten those willing with Spiritual Principles to avoid erring or defiling what is designed to BLESS.

Spiritual Laws provide a FRAMEWORK for how we can live our lives that ALIGN with our reason for being, *As It Pleases God*. Without Spiritual Alignment or constantly pleasing ourselves without corrective measures, there is misalignment by default, causing us to vibrate out of Divine Frequency instead of inside of it.

According to *The WHY Blueprint*, positive mental building blocks or Spiritual Building Blocks can benefit everyone. How? We can better understand and retain knowledge by breaking down complex information into smaller, more manageable pieces. Whether we are on the positive or Spiritual side of the block, this strategic approach can help with everything from academic studies to everyday problem-solving.

Additionally, using mental building blocks, *As It Pleases God*, can improve our ability to think critically, strategically, proactively, and creatively, enabling us to devise innovative solutions to our challenges. Overall, creating mental building blocks is a valuable tool for enhancing our cognitive abilities and achieving good success with no shame attached.

If *The WHY Blueprint* or *Blueprinted Building Blocks* are not something you feel would help achieve success, it is perfectly okay. Everyone has their own unique way of learning and problem-solving. However, it is essential to find what works best for you and stick with it with love and outright compassion, doing what you do best.

www.DrYBur.com

BUILDING BLOCK 2
Love and Compassion

The *Law of Love and Compassion* is a powerful force that can transform our lives beyond human reasoning. When we approach others with kindness, empathy, and understanding, we create a ripple effect of positivity spreading far and wide with a restorative impact. By authentically living within the constraints of the *Law of Love and Compassion*, we can build stronger relationships, improve our communities, and make a real difference in or out of the Kingdom of God.

According to the Heavenly of Heavens, we can change the world by avoiding judgment, hatred, debauchery, and violence, replacing them with a positive mindset, *As It Pleases God*. How is this possible in a hostile, negative environment? Once again, our MINDSET is the key. Why? A positive mindset is essential to effectively learning, growing, and sharing, *As It Pleases Him*. More importantly, there will always be a lesson hidden within all things, and the *Law of*

Love and Compassion makes it easier to pinpoint or glean the lesson, testing, or rerouting.

Practicing mindfulness with the *Law of Love and Compassion* involves being present in the moment while non-judgmentally observing your thoughts, actions, reactions, and words. How do we embark upon observing them? First, you must focus on developing self-awareness, self-mirroring, or self-deflection (testing or questioning yourself), which can help you recognize negative thought patterns to reframe them positively. Secondly, prioritization and time management can help you stay on track and reduce stress, positively impacting your mental status. Thirdly, your verbal and written communication skills are crucial for effective collaboration, articulation, and problem-solving. So, practicing clear and respectful communication can help keep your mental building blocks positive, productive, fruitful, and effective.

The *Law of Love and Compassion* is not a new concept, nor will it end with you. It has been expressed in various ways by different religions, philosophies, and cultures throughout history. For example, it is known as the integral Golden Rule in Christianity: *"Therefore, whatever you want men to do to you, do also to them, for this is the Law and the Prophets."* Matthew 7:12. Here are a few more, but not limited to such:

- *"For God so loved the world that He gave His only begotten Son, that whoever believes in Him should not perish but have everlasting life."* John 3:16.
- *"And now abide faith, hope, love, these three; but the greatest of these is love."* 1 Corinthians 13:13.
- *"We love Him because He first loved us."* 1 John 4:19.

- ☐ "Beloved, let us love one another, for love is of God; and everyone who loves is born of God and knows God." 1 John 4:7.
- ☐ "He who does not love does not know God, for God is love." 1 John 4:8.
- ☐ "Let love be without hypocrisy. Abhor what is evil. Cling to what is good." Romans 12:9.
- ☐ "Love suffers long and is kind; love does not envy; love does not parade itself, is not puffed up." 1 Corinthians 13:4.
- ☐ "Love does no harm to a neighbor; therefore love is the fulfillment of the law." Romans 13:10.
- ☐ "A new commandment I give to you, that you love one another; as I have loved you, that you also love one another." John 13:34.
- ☐ "And above all things have fervent love for one another, for 'love will cover a multitude of sins.' " 1 Peter 4:8.
- ☐ "But I say to you, love your enemies, bless those who curse you, do good to those who hate you, and pray for those who spitefully use you and persecute you." Matthew 5:44.
- ☐ "Finally, all of you be of one mind, having compassion for one another; love as brothers, be tenderhearted, be courteous." 1 Peter 3:8.

Why is The *Law of Love and Compassion* essential in the Eye of God? Simply put, we are all connected as ONE. Without loving others, we cannot fully love ourselves properly, even if we are really into ourselves. Why? The Divine Spark of Greatness resides within us, and we are designed to share it with others, even if we feel they do not deserve it.

Nonetheless, this Spiritual Law's most amazing transformative aspect is to give, expecting nothing in return.

Why? It removes the false expectations we can easily impose upon others. Listen to me and listen well: False expectations create our disappointments. Without expectations, we have fewer disappointments by default, reducing hurt, trauma, and unforgiveness by default.

Should we not set expectations? First and foremost, we should set expectations for ourselves, *As It Pleases God*, spreading outwardly and living by example using the Fruits of the Spirit and behaving Christlike. Secondly, we must allow others to be who they are. And thirdly, we should not violate the free will of another. If people are going to treat us right, they will. If they want to speak to us kindly, they will. If they want to respect us, they will. We do not need to make them! The *Law of Love and Compassion* will save a lot of time, stress, and disappointments!

What about our children? Should we not set expectations for them? They are a representation of our seeds sown in and out of season. We are to train them, not expect them! Why? It removes the assumptions. *"Train up a child in the way he should go, And when he is old he will not depart from it."* Proverbs 22:6. Knowing and expecting are two different things in the Eye of God that must be redirected back to ourselves, *As It Pleases Him*, and not to please ourselves or others.

How can we practice the *Law of Love and Compassion* without feeling like a wimp or simp? Here are a few suggestions, but not limited to such:

- ☐ Be mindful of your thoughts, words, actions, and reactions, keeping them positive, productive, and fruitful.

- ☐ Before you say or do something, ask yourself: 'Is this loving? Is this compassionate? Is it kind? Is this helpful? Is it positively fruitful? Is it righteous?' If not, then refrain from it or find a better way to express yourself or do what you do.

- ☐ Listen actively and empathetically to others. Try to understand their perspective, feelings, and needs.

- ☐ Do not judge or try to fix people. Just be present with them and offer your support and words of encouragement.

- ☐ Express gratitude and appreciation for others. Thank them for their contributions, acknowledge their strengths, and celebrate their achievements. Tell them how much they mean to you and how they improve your life.

- ☐ Forgive yourself and others. Do not hold on to resentment, anger, unforgiveness, or guilt. They only hurt you, preventing you from healing and moving forward in the Spirit of Excellence.

- ☐ Learn from your mistakes, apologize when needed, let go of the past, and keep it moving.

- ☐ Serve others with generosity and kindness. Look for opportunities to help others in need, whether it is by giving your time, money, skills, or resources.

- ☐ Share your Spiritual Gifts, Calling, Talents, and Creativity with the world.

- ☐ Make sure you are smiling, complimenting others, and offering goodwill gestures.

- ☐ Practice self-care and self-compassion. Do not neglect your own well-being. You must take care of yourself, Mentally, Physically, Emotionally, Spiritually, and Financially.

- ☐ Treat yourself and others with respect and love. Please do not be too hard on yourself or others. Nor should you compare yourself to others or compare them to others.

- ☐ You are enough just as you are, and they are enough just as they are, because everything you need is already within you or them. Remember, you cannot change anyone; you must change yourself and live by example, *As It Pleases God.*

Notably, these are practicalities of utilizing the *Law of Love and Compassion* daily. By doing so, you will improve your joy, happiness, harmony, peace, and fulfillment, and inspire others to do likewise. Plus, you will become a positive force to be reckoned with, having a memorable impact.

The *Law of Love and Compassion* is not something you have to do; it is something you are. It is Divinely your true human nature and Spiritual Essence working together for your good. So embrace it fully and live it authentically. "And let the peace of God rule in your hearts, to which also you were called in one body; and be thankful." Colossians 3:15.

BUILDING BLOCK 3

Attraction

The *Law of Attraction* is a powerful Divine Conceptual Magnet that has existed since the beginning of time. Most know about this Spiritual Law, but do not fully understand its WHY and how to make it work in their favor in *Building Their Own Table*. As a part of *The WHY Blueprint*, we need this Spiritual Law to work on our behalf, not against us; therefore, we must fully understand it from God's Divine Perspective.

The basic premise of misconception is that if we think positively and focus on our goals, we will manifest them into reality. Unfortunately, if our goals, desires, and dreams do not align with our Predestined Blueprint, we can cause more harm than good. We cannot use the *Law of Attraction* selfishly, unwisely, or debaucherously. Why? We may become Spiritually Blind, Deaf, or Mute, making us stiff-necked, dull, traumatized, or unusable.

The *Law of Attraction* has two sides: positive or negative, right or wrong, just or unjust, righteous or unrighteous, and so on. For this reason, we must determine WHAT we are attracting, WHY, and which side of the scale it falls on. By not knowing the facts associated with this Spiritual Law, we can 'get got' while appearing right in our own eyes, causing the *Law of Attraction* to become a *Law of Repellant*. Is this a Spiritual Law? Of course.

There will always be two sides to any Spiritual Law, similar to every word having its opposite. *"Therefore, to you who believe, He is precious; but to those who are disobedient, 'The stone which the builders rejected has become the chief cornerstone,' and 'A stone of stumbling and a rock of offense.' They stumble, being disobedient to the word, to which they also were appointed."* 1 Peter 2:7-8. When using the *Law of Attraction*, we must exercise caution in what or who we reject to fill a temporary need or void. Why? The cornerstones and rocks of offense are real.

It is often said, 'The same people we meet on our way up will be the same ones we will encounter on our way down.' Therefore, we should treat everyone respectfully and kindly, even if they did us wrong, played dirty, or threw us under the bus. As the *Law of Attraction* is intentionally or unintentionally set in motion, it is always best to use the Fruits of the Spirit and behave Christlike.

By aligning our thoughts and emotions with our desires, *As It Pleases God*, we can create the life we truly want. Is this Biblical? Absolutely! *"Trust in the Lord with all your heart, and lean not on your own understanding; In all your ways acknowledge Him, And He shall direct your paths."* Proverbs 3:5-6. On the other hand, if we leave Him out of our equational efforts, we can inadvertently cause our lives to become a living nightmare. Why? Just because we want something or someone, it does not make it suitable for us. Nor does it make it right in the Eye of God.

According to the Heavenly of Heavens, it is essential to remember that the *Law of Attraction* is not about wishful thinking or just hoping for the best. It requires positive action, effort, proactiveness, and a willingness to take risks. Really? Yes, really. *"But seek first the kingdom of God and His righteousness, and all these things shall be added to you."* Matthew 6:33.

But with persistence and faith in ourselves, we can achieve anything we set our minds to do, especially if it aligns with our Divine Blueprinted Purpose. What if it does not align? We will become distracted, delayed, dismayed, or detoured with a cycle of déjà vu, where our history will repeat itself until we get the lessons we need to learn. In addition, we will also experience anxiety, stress, and unrest within the conscience, causing the psyche to want more and more like a bottomless pit. Why? It is due to the sense of entitlement without putting in the work or Spiritually Tilling our own ground.

The bottom line is that in the Eye of God, He is looking for Spiritual Fruits and Christlike Character, mainly when Spiritually Manifesting with the *Law of Attraction*. Conversely, we associate it with material gain, forgetting all about our germinating seeds, causing a snare for us. How is this possible? *"But those who desire to be rich fall into temptation and a snare, and into many foolish and harmful lusts which drown men in destruction and perdition. For the love of money is a root of all kinds of evil, for which some have strayed from the faith in their greediness, and pierced themselves through with many sorrows."* 1 Timothy 6:9-10.

If we use mangled or debauched fruits with atrocious character, we will attract that into whatever we hope for. As a result, we blame God and become disappointed, frustrated, and confused, as if the *Law of Attraction* does not work. When, in all actuality, it was attracted from within first, and then spread outwardly.

Our reality will playback what is from within or based upon our seeded core. For example, we will attract a chaotic situation if we lack inner peace. Without humility, we will attract people, places, and things to pump our ego with a letdown behind closed doors. We will attract hateful people if we are hateful, causing more compounded trauma because we do not know how to deal with ourselves or them, *As It Pleases God.* For this reason, when dealing with the *Law of Attraction*, "*Be anxious for nothing, but in everything by prayer and supplication, with thanksgiving, let your requests be made known to God; and the peace of God, which surpasses all understanding, will guard your hearts and minds through Christ Jesus.*" Philippians 4:6-7.

Regardless of where we are in life or what we have going on, God is looking for contentment, gratitude, and understanding with a focus on Him, our Spiritual Values (Fruits and Character), and our Predestined Blueprint. Without knowing our reason for being, becoming a work-in-progress to complete our Divine Mission, or becoming a better person, *As It Pleases Him*, all else is vanity (fleeting or temporary). Really? Yes, really! Please allow me to Align Spiritually: "*Then I looked on all the works that my hands had done and on the labor in which I had toiled; and indeed all was vanity and grasping for the wind. There was no profit under the sun.*" Ecclesiastes 2:11.

When *Building Your Own Table* or activating the *Law of Attraction*, ensure you incorporate your *Spirit to Spirit* Connection with your Heavenly Father into your equational efforts. Why? True fulfillment can only come from having an authentic connection with the Holy Trinity while working on your Predestined Blueprint, doing what you were called to do.

www.DrYBur.com

BUILDING BLOCK 4

Seedtime and Harvest

The *Law of Seedtime and Harvest* is another powerful concept often associated with the *Law of Attraction*. Still, it is slightly different because it allows us to regraft, replant, and reverse our seeds before harvest time. More importantly, it was a Promise to Noah, *"While the earth remains, seedtime and harvest, cold and heat, winter and summer, and day and night shall not cease."* Genesis 8:22.

No one or nothing is exempt from the *Law of Seedtime and Harvest*, even if we think we are. It applies to every aspect of our lives, such as finances, health, relationships, career, and Spirituality. More importantly, it also implies a delay between sowing and reaping, giving us time to undo, redo, or untie whatever with whomever.

Why do we get time to undo, redo, or untie? First, it helps us to build mercy, compassion, and understanding for ourselves and others. Secondly, we do not come straight out of the gate perfect. For example, we will never see a child born into this world as a full-grown adult; if we do, run! And thirdly, we are designed to become better, stronger, and wiser with time and practice. For this reason, we have Divine Grace working in our favor, especially if we Spiritually Till our own ground and become a work-in-progress, making our best attempt to do and say the right things, *As It Pleases God.*

The cycle of planting and reaping or sowing and reaping is the same, but we often forget about our actions, reactions, thoughts, beliefs, and words being seeds. So, before going any further, here is what we must know: *"Do not be deceived, God is not mocked; for whatever a man sows, that he will also reap. For he who sows to his flesh will of the flesh reap corruption, but he who sows to the Spirit will of the Spirit reap everlasting life. And let us not grow weary while doing good, for in due season we shall reap if we do not lose heart."* Galatians 6:7-9.

What is the purpose of dealing with the *Law of Seedtime and Harvest*? This Spiritual Law is prewired in our DNA, even if we do not know about it or understand its implications. Then again, some hide under the *Law of Grace* to do nothing or as a cover-up to avoid any form of recourse, but it does not nullify the seeds, roots, or fruits involved. Without repentance, it only causes us to point the finger, lie, or become fake, ruining our authenticity when the harvest comes in.

By taking responsibility for our actions, reactions, thoughts, words, beliefs, biases, and making choices that align with the Fruits of the Spirit and Christlike Character, we can create positive life experiences, even if we have messed up royally. For example, I have made many mistakes and bad decisions while outright disobeying God's Divine Will. Even though I knew better and had the full instructions of what I needed to do and why, I chose not to do better at the time. Why not? I wanted to do what I wanted, and it would take too long to do what God wanted me to do.

Still, amid my erring and resistance, God did not give up on me. With a charactorial overhaul and regrafting of my Mind, Body, and Soul, *As It Pleased Him*, I am here providing the Spiritual Illumination for the next man, leaving no willing person behind. What does this mean? I do not force-feed anyone; I share the information without any strings attached. If it is for someone, it will penetrate, doing what it is designed to do. If not, I keep it moving in the Spirit of Excellence to the next in line without convincing anyone.

Why would I not spend more time convincing? We do not need to convince someone to help them. They must want it for themselves, Spiritually Tilling their own ground, *As It Pleases God*. When dealing with the *Law of Seedtime and Harvest*, no one can put in the work for us...they can guide, mentor, or inspire, but they cannot use the sweat from another man's brow. It must come from their own efforts to determine what they reap or their harvesting capacity. Is this Biblical? I would have it no other way. *"In the sweat of your face you shall eat bread till you return to the ground, for out of it you were taken; for dust you are, and to dust you shall return."* Genesis 3:19.

What if we take the easy way out? In the Eye of God, there is no easy way regarding the seeds sown in or out of season; they will come home to roost when we least expect them. Once again, it behooves us to always keep our seeds positive, productive, and fruitful, *As It Pleases God*, using the Fruits of the Spirit and behaving Christlike.

According to the Heavenly of Heavens, it is crucial to remember that the *Law of Seedtime and Harvest* is not about perfection or living in fear of making mistakes. Even the seed must crack out of its shell to become what it needs to be; therefore, we will experience the same. It is about learning from our mistakes, growing, taking ownership of our choices, and striving to be the best version of ourselves, according to our Predestined Blueprint.

BUILDING BLOCK 5
Forgiveness

The *Law of Forgiveness* is one of the most overlooked and avoided Spiritual Laws known to man. Still, it is the most liberating and healing Spiritual Law, bridging the gap between our reality and Divine Destiny or our ability to repent and forgive. When seeking the Hand of God, we must cleanse the Mind, Body, and Soul of unforgiveness. Why? Simply put, *"For if you forgive men their trespasses, your heavenly Father will also forgive you. But if you do not forgive men their trespasses, neither will your Father forgive your trespasses."* Matthew 6:14-15. Forgiveness is not for them; it is for us!

Holding on to unforgiveness will cause our Spiritual Fruits to spoil, contaminating the fruits of another and causing judgmentalism to consume us. How can we become judgmentally consumed as Believers? If we are negative, rude, jealous, envious, prideful, greedy, arrogant, covetous, or competitive, judgmentalism feeds them all from one unforgiving seed.

When dealing with negative characteristics, we must first check the unforgiving seeds of trauma, conditioning, or bias. According to the Heavenly of Heavens, no one is exempt from negativity, even if we think we are or believe we have tough skin. For example, invisible dust particles get on us and the things around us without our noticing until they become visibly compounded. The goal is to recognize the invisible particles of unforgiveness and negativity, know what to do about them, and why we are doing it.

Why is paying attention so important when dealing with unforgiveness? Most often, we repent but avoid forgiving. Then again, we say we have forgiven, but our words, thoughts, beliefs, and actions say otherwise. On the other hand, we may forgive out of custom while not repenting regarding our role in the situation, circumstance, or event. We can call this a Catch-22, yet we can also call it a Catch-23. In all simplicity, Catch-23 is living by Psalm 23.

Forgiving can be difficult, primarily when we have been wronged, used, abused, outed, or made to feel like boo-boo the fool. However, when *Building Your Own Table*, Psalm 23 can provide consolation for the struggling and weary soul. It says:

"The Lord is my shepherd; I shall not want. He makes me to lie down in green pastures; He leads me beside the still waters. He restores my soul; He leads me in the paths of righteousness For His name's sake. Yea, though I walk through the valley of the shadow of death, I will fear no evil; For You are with me; Your rod and Your staff, they comfort me. You prepare a table before me in the presence of my enemies; You anoint my head with oil; My cup runs over. Surely goodness and mercy shall follow me All the days of my life; And I will dwell in the house of the Lord Forever."

Does it work? Absolutely! I am living proof. Forgiveness has become my Spiritual Weapon to keep negativity from attaching itself to my Predestined Blueprinted Purpose. More importantly, it keeps my Spiritual Fruits intact and on point, enabling me to know what fruit to use, when to apply it, how to use it, why I am using it, where to do so, and if I need to use multiple ones.

For example, when using the Fruits of the Spirit, I may not need to use the Fruit of Love but Self-Control. Then again, with someone else, I may need to apply them all: Love, Joy, Peace, Patience, Kindness, Goodness, Faithfulness, Gentleness, and Self-Control. The bottom line is that I need to know what to use at the right time, and I need the Holy Trinity involved to apply them correctly with Spiritual Discernment. So, I cannot allow unforgiveness to block my Spiritual Channels of Divine Communication.

Forgiveness is not always easy, but it is necessary. Why? Holding onto anger, bitterness, and resentment only hurts us. By letting go, we free ourselves from the negative emotions, thoughts, traumas, and beliefs that keep us trapped in the past or a rut.

What if someone takes our forgiveness for a weakness? Continue to forgive them. Here is what we must know: "*Then Peter came to Him and said, 'Lord, how often shall my brother sin against me, and I forgive him? Up to seven times?' Jesus said to him, 'I do not say to you, up to seven times, but up to seventy times seven.'* " Matthew 18:21-22. Forgiving helps us to exercise wisdom to avoid certain traps, yokes, and distractions or to stand up for ourselves, knowing when to hold, fold, or walk away.

The Law of Forgiveness DOES NOT make us weak; it makes us STRONG. In the Eye of God, not dealing with the emotions of unforgiveness or the lack of self-control weakens us. Forgiveness does not mean we should put ourselves in harm's way; it means we will forgive and keep moving in the Spirit of Excellence.

Exercising the *Law of Forgiveness* grants us proactive grace. What does this mean? We all make mistakes and need forgiveness; therefore, if we proactively give it, we can proactively receive it. Really? Yes, really! *"If we confess our sins, He is faithful and just to forgive us our sins and to cleanse us from all unrighteousness."* 1 John 1:9.

The *Law of Forgiveness* cleanses the psyche of its damaging impurities. Thus, we must allow it to do what it is designed to do, and if we hold on to what is hurting us, then we cannot lay the blame elsewhere.

Unfortunately, according to the Heavenly of Heavens, we can cancel out the lower Spiritual Laws by not enforcing this HIGHER ONE. Really? Yes, really! It can block our *Spirit to Spirit* Connection with our Heavenly Father, cause us to misuse the Blood of Jesus, and blaspheme against the Holy Spirit. Why? God weighs the heart, and if our heart is weighed down with unforgiveness, it contaminates our intentions while appearing right in our own eyes, causing us to pray amissly or operate selfishly.

Regardless of our situation or circumstance, FORGIVE! Our Spiritual Growth depends on it. Before moving to the *Law of Abundance*, remember this: *"And be kind to one another, tenderhearted, forgiving one another, even as God in Christ forgave you."* Ephesians 4:32.

BUILDING BLOCK 6

Abundance

The *Law of Abundance* is not a magic formula or pill; it is a MINDSET encouraging us to focus on abundance rather than scarcity, while knowing everything is already. For this reason, we must enter into a state of abundance by aligning our thoughts, emotions, words, actions, and demeanor with vibrational abundance to usher in what rightly belongs to us.

In or out of the yearning for Divine Abundance, we all have needs, wants, and desires; however, a threat will always be associated with them. For this reason, we must develop a mindset that PLEASES God. Why must we live with threats? It builds our faith, trust, hope, and dependence upon God, removing the elements of selfish dominion from the inside out. What does this mean? We naturally tend to dominate people, places, and things without correct information, leaving God out of the equation as if He does not exist.

Being that we are not created as a one-pony rodeo, what makes us money does not mean we are in God's Divine

Will...there is always more! According to the Heavenly of Heavens, our more may not be the same as God's. Why? One leads us to the PIT, and the other to the KINGDOM. Yet, we must know the difference to cause the *Law of Abundance* to work in our favor as a Blessing, not a yokable leash or curse.

How can having more create curses, bondage, or yokes? The chokehold of more, more, and more will cause us to 'get got' by the internal greed of more money, more love, more success, more women or men, more happiness, and so on. All of these are hidden under the lust of the eyes, the lusts of the flesh, and the pride of life. The more, more, and more mentality of ungratefulness also comes with more problems that money cannot solve; therefore, it is wise to put people, places, and things into their proper perspective, *As It Pleases God.*

According to our Predestined Blueprint or reason for being, God will provide when we are in Purpose on purpose. What does this mean? We must search for or seek out our Divine Purpose instead of just existing, taking up space on a constant cycle of déjà vu, doing nothing, and benefiting no one but ourselves. *"But be doers of the word, and not hearers only, deceiving yourselves."* James 1:22.

Once we wholeheartedly align ourselves, *As It Pleases God*, we can legitimately quote this scripture back to Him, *"And we know that all things work together for good to those who love God, to those who are the called according to His purpose."* Romans 8:28. What is so special about this? Our Divine Blueprint has its own set of provisions.

In the *Law of Abundance*, if we add God into the equation, *As It Pleases Him*, where He guides, He provides. Is this Biblical? I would have it no other way, *"And my God shall supply all your needs according to His riches in glory by Christ Jesus."*

Philippians 4:19. Can He really supply for us? If He provided for the Children of Israel in the desert for 40 years with manna and water while they complained, bickered, fussed, fought, and lacked faith, how much more can He do for us if we reverse-engineer where they went wrong?

God is faithful and has more than enough of everything for us, especially when we are grateful, obedient, humble, non-confrontational, peaceful, proactive, and helpful. To have what we need, repeat this daily: *"Our father in heaven, hallowed be your name. Your Kingdom come. Your will be done on earth as it is in Heaven. Give us this day our daily bread. And forgive us our debts, as we forgive our debtors. And do not lead us into temptation, but deliver us from the evil one. For yours is the Kingdom and the power and the glory forever. Amen."* Matthew 6:9-13.

The *Law of Abundance* is a powerful way to attract more strength, wealth, happiness, wisdom, knowledge, understanding, and good success. With a mindset adjustment from scarcity to abundance, *As It Pleases God*, we can overcome limiting beliefs, fears, and doubts holding us back from achieving whatever, with whomever.

The mindset of the *Law of Abundance* is not about being greedy, prideful, or selfish. It is about recognizing your true potential and value, being grateful for what you have, and sharing with others. How can we make this Spiritual Law work without offense, unwise defense, or erring? It will vary from person to person, situation to situation, trauma to trauma, culture to culture, and so on. Nonetheless, here are a few steps to cultivate the *Law of Abundance* mindset, *As It Pleases God*, but not limited to such:

- ☐ Be clear about what you want and why you want it.

- ☐ Write down your visions, dreams, desires, wants, and needs in your Spiritual Journal, affirming them daily.
- ☐ Practice gratitude for what you already have.
- ☐ Express appreciation for the people, places, things, and opportunities.
- ☐ Replace negative thoughts with positive ones.
- ☐ Focus on the possibilities and solutions, not the problems and obstacles.
- ☐ Be flexible, adaptable, and open to new opportunities with Divine Discernment at the forefront.
- ☐ Take action towards your goals.
- ☐ Trust the Holy Trinity to guide, train, protect, provide, and support you.
- ☐ Do not let fear or doubt stop you. Keep moving in the Spirit of Excellence.
- ☐ Celebrate your achievements and acknowledge your progress.
- ☐ Reward yourself for your efforts.
- ☐ Learn from your mistakes and share the wisdom with others.
- ☐ Be open to receiving. Do not reject or resist it; embrace it with joy, peacefulness, and gratitude, allowing God to filter out what you do not need.
- ☐ Leave no stone unturned. Remember, the Blessing or Promise will never appear as such; it may come as a seed or a diamond in the rough.

The *Law of Abundance* is designed to transform your life, taking you to the next level of Divine Greatness. Once we become true to ourselves, our Predestined Blueprint will unveil the Heavenly Truths about what we already possess from within.

BUILDING BLOCK 7

Detachment

Do you know when it is time to let go? Are you afraid of parting ways with someone you love? Do you fear loneliness? Are you ready to embrace your inner peace? Does the presence of someone or something cause painful triggers? The *Law of Detachment* is a Spiritual Principle encouraging us to let go of our attachments to toxic people, places, things, and specific outcomes that do not align with our Divine Blueprint.

Most often, we may not know that we are toxic or that our situation is toxic. Why? We all appear right in our own eyes and often do not like being on the losing end. Although we are all subjected to this proclivity, we can reverse-engineer it to create a win-win. How? By knowing the difference between Spiritual Alignment versus misalignment.

How can we determine what's what and who is whom? We must usher in the Holy Trinity (The Father, Son, and Holy Spirit), use the Fruits of the Spirit, and behave

Christlike as a Spiritual Filter for ourselves, spreading outwardly. Why? It develops our Spiritual Compass and Conscience. Therefore, *"Set your mind on things above, not on things on the earth."* Colossians 3:2.

The beauty of letting go is letting God take the wheel as He Spiritually Calibrates us to know what or who is for us, and who and what is not. Doing so will change the trajectory of our lives, transforming the Mind, Body, and Soul, allowing our Spirit Man to come forth. With this mindset, *As It Pleases God*, what belongs to us will be, and what is not cannot remain, period.

What if we make a mistake in choosing? We all make mistakes and are subjected to human error. *"Therefore do not worry about tomorrow, for tomorrow will worry about its own things. Sufficient for the day is its own trouble."* Matthew 6:34. Once we are in Purpose on purpose according to our Predestined Blueprint, we do not lose! With this type of Spiritual Discernment from being under our Divinely Blueprinted Covering, we only gain wisdom, insight, lessons, instructions, understanding, pruning, and redirection. And our responsibility is to document it.

What if we choose not to document? We have free will to do whatever we so desire. Thus, by opting out of documenting, we get limited access to what is Divine, creating trust and selfishness issues. Why? If God trusts us to document our Testimony as a Testament for the next man, He will open up the Floodgates of Wisdom. On the other hand, if the information stops with us, He will close it, leaving us to our own devices, causing what should be detach to attach like leeches and ticks, sucking the life out of us.

What is the big deal about documenting? Out of all God's creative efforts, we are the ones whom He granted the ability to document, and what do we do? We decline to use this Spiritual Tool of Greatness to give back to the Kingdom for the greater good. Listen, documenting is our life-giving Spiritual Tool that can be used with the *Law of Detachment* to change lives.

When using the *Law of Detachment*, I want to know the reason WHY. According to *The WHY Blueprint*, 'What Hurts You is What Heals You.' And if you are detaching from something or someone, there is a reason for doing so...and this is what I want to know. Why do I need to know? It is a part of your story to help the next person overcome the accusers. Is this Biblical? *"And they overcame him by the blood of the Lamb and by the word of their testimony, and they did not love their lives to the death."* Revelation 12:11.

Ultimately, the *Law of Detachment* reminds us that our circumstances do not define us. Regardless of how life appears to the naked eye, we have the power and freedom to choose how we think, feel, and respond, as well as what we do. *"And do not be conformed to this world, but be transformed by the renewing of your mind, that you may prove what is that good and acceptable and perfect will of God."* Romans 12:2.

As you get into the habit of documenting in your *Spirit to Spirit* alone time with God, listed below are a few ways to detach yourself, but not limited to such:

- ☐ Learn how to say 'NO' kindly.
- ☐ Practice meditation to help clear your mind.
- ☐ Detach from negative thoughts by replacing them with positive ones.
- ☐ Cultivate a sense of gratitude.

- ☐ Focus on what you have rather than what you lack.
- ☐ Set healthy boundaries.
- ☐ Avoid becoming too attached to the opinions of others.
- ☐ Do not accept toxic behaviors within yourself or with others. Politely excuse yourself.
- ☐ Practice letting go of your expectations.
- ☐ Allow people, places, and things to unfold naturally.
- ☐ Learn to accept things without trying to control or manipulate everything.
- ☐ Practice forgiveness to release any negative emotions or attachments.
- ☐ Let go of any negative or limiting beliefs.
- ☐ Shut down all negative self-talk or mental chatter.
- ☐ Practice humility.
- ☐ Focus on your own personal growth and development.
- ☐ Do not compare yourself to others; your Spiritual Journey is uniquely yours.
- ☐ Focus on your purpose, creativity, talents, and passion rather than external validation.
- ☐ Use the Fruits of the Spirit, even if you have to create a checklist for yourself.
- ☐ Behave Christlike, even if someone rubs you the wrong way.

By not using the *Law of Detachment*, you may struggle with distractions and lack time management skills. Plus, there are times when you may have to step back, detaching from everything and everyone to help you make sense of yourself and your life. According to the Heavenly of Heavens, it is okay to detach or prune occasionally; it is perfectly normal. What is NOT normal is NOT to do it!

To promote growth, you must cut away dead or unproductive people, places, and things. Please allow me to align the following: *"I am the true vine, and My Father is the vinedresser. Every branch in Me that does not bear fruit He takes away; and every branch that bears fruit He prunes, that it may bear more fruit."* John 15:1-2.

Why is it so crucial to detach from negativity, *As It Pleases God*? *"But you are a chosen generation, a royal priesthood, a holy nation, His own special people, that you may proclaim the praises of Him who called you out of darkness into His marvelous light."* 1 Peter 2:9.

www.DrYBur.com

BUILDING BLOCK 8

Intention

What are your intentions? Do you streamline your intents? How do your intentions affect your life? How do your intentions affect others? Most of us do not realize there is a Spiritual Law guarding and governing our intentions. Although God weighs our intents or motives, most often, we do not, contributing to its misuse.

How do we misuse the *Law of Intention*? It will vary from person to person, situation to situation, trauma to trauma, culture to culture, and so on. However, we often unawaringly interchange intents and motives. How so? Motives refer to the driving force, seed, or underlying reasons why we would do something. Intent refers to the purpose or goal behind our actions to achieve a desired outcome, similar to watering the seed with the intent for it to grow into a plant, tree, or bush. Knowing the difference between the two helps us better understand how we think, react, behave, speak, and make decisions.

The *Law of Intention* is a principle emphasizing the importance of setting clear intentions for what we want to achieve, creating alignment. What does this mean? It is similar to having MIND-EYE COORDINATION, where our thoughts align with what we see. Whereas the *Law of Intention* incorporates the whole gamut, such as:

- ☐ Mind-Eye Coordination.
- ☐ Hand-Eye Coordination.
- ☐ Heart-Eye Coordination.
- ☐ Word-Eye Coordination.
- ☐ Action-Eye Coordination.
- ☐ Ear-Eye Coordination.

The heart must align with our vision to ensure our actions follow suit. When our intentions do not match our goals, thoughts, or desires, we will find ourselves all over the place, lacking consistency, appearing scattered, pulling for straws, or plugging and playing. Why? When the mind says one thing, our actions say something else, and our heart tells us a different story, it creates confusion within the human psyche, spreading outwardly.

Have you ever been around someone having a conversation, and once it was over, you walked away more confused than ever? Well, now you know why! Therefore, when conversing, it is okay to state your intent if there is one. Why? Clarity is one of the critical elements of becoming an excellent conversationalist, listening is the second factor, and understanding is the third.

Most put becoming a good listener at the top of their list; however, clarity is primal in the Eye of God. Is this Biblical? *"So likewise you, unless you utter by the tongue words easy to* understand, how will it be known what is spoken? For you will be speaking into the air." 1 Corinthians 14:9.

Listening helps us to increase our learning and knowledge, Mentally, Physically, Emotionally, and Spiritually. What does this mean? We must listen to understand, and we must understand before responding to keep us from looking like boo-boo the fool who lacks discipline or understanding.

When I encounter someone running their mouth without formal discretion, all types of red flags go up. Why? We must listen to learn, not speak without understanding. Proverbs 1:5 says, *"A wise man will hear and increase learning, and a man of understanding will attain wise counsel."* And, *"He who answers a matter before he hears it, it is folly and shame to him."* Proverbs 18:13.

To understand correctly, we must learn how to ask the right questions. Unfortunately, there is no way to activate the *Law of Intention* without the Spiritual Basics, *As It Pleases God*. All else is considered self-intent or selfish motives, eventually leading to folly. How does folly get in the picture? Without gaining clarity through listening, learning, understanding, and querying, the mind will not align with the heart, causing our hands to falter, misalign, or fumble.

What if we are successful and have it going on? I am not here to judge anyone's level of success or status; I am looking for Spiritual Alignment, *As It Pleases God*. Plus, what most people consider success may not be what they proclaim. God uses a different measuring stick based on our capacity. Really? Yes, really! *"But the Lord said to Samuel, 'Do not look at his appearance or at his physical stature, because I have refused him. For the Lord does not see as man sees; for man looks at the outward appearance, but the Lord looks at the heart.'"* 1 Samuel 16:7.

For example, I am held to a higher accountability than the average person who knows nothing about Spiritual Principles, Laws, Protocols, and Blueprints. Plus, my Divine Mission differs from the next person's, requiring increased and intense Spiritual Training. However, the Fruits of the Spirit and Christlike Character are the same across the board. For this reason, I look for the Fruits of the Spirit and Christlike Character, regardless of what someone says or does. Why? They reveal the *Laws of Intent* by default, letting me know if it is self-intent or Godly Intent. It also indicates whether they have Kingdom Potential or are a work-in-progress.

What if we have our own way of doing things? Then my question would be, 'How is that working for you?' 'Is it bringing you in Purpose on purpose?' 'Do you have your Divine Blueprint documented?'

Why all the questionable queries? God is looking for our heart posture. Proverbs 17:3 says, *"The refining pot is for silver and the furnace for gold, but the Lord tests the hearts."* When tested, tried, and placed in the fiery furnace like Shadrach, Meshach, and Abednego in Daniel 3:16-28, it determines the sayers, seers, doers, and liars. If we do not know where we fall on this scale, we will become a slippery slope from the inside out. Why? The Mind, Body, Soul, and Spirit will be tested, and if we fail, it is back to the drawing board or cycle of déjà vu.

What if we pass the test? We are off to the next round, preparing for the next level of Spiritual Milk to Meat. The bottom line is that we need to grow *As It Pleases God*, not as it pleases ourselves. What is up with all the levels and ranks of understanding? According to the Heavenly of Heavens, *"Wisdom is the principal thing; therefore get wisdom. And in all your getting, get understanding."* Proverbs 4:7. The *Law of Intention* encourages us to take responsibility and action, or proactively prepare. Rather than waiting for things to happen or having things fall into our laps without effort, we can do our due diligence.

"Brethren, do not be children in understanding; however, in malice be babes, but in understanding be mature." 1 Corinthians 14:20. In maturing in the *Law of Intention*, here are a few things you need, but are not limited to such:

- ☐ **Clarity**: You need to be clear about the specific intention of what you want to create or experience. The more detailed and precise your intention is, the more likely it is to manifest.

- ☐ **Commitment**: You must commit to your intention and act as if it is already done. You must align your beliefs, words, thoughts, and behaviors with your intention. Avoid any doubts, fears, contradictions, or negative motives.

- ☐ **Consistency**: You must maintain your focus and attention on your intention. Avoid distractions, naysayers, and dream destroyers.

- ☐ **Gratitude**: Express gratitude for your intention. Gratitude is a powerful emotion attracting more of what you want.

- ☐ **Surrender**: You need to surrender to the process of the WHAT and WHY. You do not need to worry about how-to, when-to, or where-to. You just need to align, document, prepare, let go, and allow it to happen.

Ultimately, the *Law of Intention* reminds us that we have the power to bring our Predestined Blueprint alive, doing what we were called to do.

Building Block 9
Unity

Do you feel divided? Is it difficult to get on one accord with yourself or others? Do you have a hard time coming together with others? Are you consumed with a hidden power struggle from within? Are you controlling? Today, we face many challenges and conflicts threatening to divide us, undermine our common goals, shut us down, or silence us. Whether personal, political, social, economic, or environmental, we often find ourselves in situations where we must choose sides, defend our positions, or scratch our heads in dismay. All these lead to damaged or strained relationships and faltering well-being, causing us to question our ability to unite.

With or without the underlying questions, unification is a part of our DNA, having the capacity to cross-gene itself. What does this mean? The *Law of Unity* is within us, even if we do not recognize it. Yet, with our cross-genes, we can cause animals to adapt to our nature and understand our language without speaking it verbally. Everything we need is already within us. We are the only species of God's Divine Creation that do not recognize this Divine Trait, only to be used by everything outside of us.

Animals know us better than we know ourselves. How do they know us? We are Spiritual Beings having a human experience, refusing to operate as such. Meanwhile, they (meaning animals) must use their Spiritual Tools and Instincts to stay alive. With one slip, it is over for them; therefore, they must know us.

We have grace and mercy in the milking stages, refusing to develop them into Divine Meat or Spiritually Unite. Then, we have the nerve to seek power or seek control over people, places, and things with lower vibrations of grace and mercy without a Spiritual Upgrade, *As It Pleases God*. As a result, we are left to our own devices, sweeping the *Law of Unity* under the rug, while secretly thinking He has abandoned or failed us.

How do lower vibrations affect our ability to unite? When operating on lower frequencies, we become Spiritually Blind, Deaf, and Mute, not knowing the difference between the Voice of God, our internal voice, or the enemy. Therefore, we think everyone and everything is against us, provoking us or causing our issues, not realizing we are operating at a bond-breaking deficit.

Underestimating and overlooking the *Law of Unity* has caused us to downplay our Divine Nature, triggering our Spiritual Receptors or Compass to warp, preventing us from operating at a High Frequency, *As It Pleases God*.

How do we know what frequency we are operating on? In the Eye of God, it is initially determined by our fruits, character, thoughts, words, behaviors, reactions, and proactiveness. Secondly, it is determined by which side of the conductor we are on. For example, positive or negative side, right or wrong side, just or unjust side, righteous or unrighteous side, and so on. Thirdly, it is determined by who runs the show...is God running it, or are we running it? Regardless of our choice, know this: *"Therefore we make it our aim, whether present or absent, to be well pleasing to Him."* 2 Corinthians 5:9.

The *Law of Unity* Spiritual Principle emphasizes coming together as ONE. What is the importance of becoming ONE? We are all interconnected. Unity is not about agreeing on everything, ignoring our differences, or whitewashing our issues. It is about finding common ground, working together for the greater good, and communicating effectively while respecting and appreciating our diversity.

The *Law of Unity* helps us overcome obstacles, solve problems, create opportunities, make positive changes, support each other, learn from one another, and grow together. Doing so cultivates a sense of purpose, passion, and bonding, helping our Divine Blueprint to come forth. How? Once we activate our people skills, *As It Pleases God*, it gives us more leverage than those who are repulsive, who are hard to deal with, or who are complainers instead of doers.

In the Eye of God, we cannot go wrong in inspiring, motivating, cultivating, and empowering each other. More importantly, it reduces violence, prejudice, and discrimination, promoting peace, justice, and kindness. Above all, when we feed God's sheep, *As It Pleases Him*, He will move Heaven and Earth to feed us or ensure we have what we need to complete our Divine Mission.

The Power of Unity is undeniably the key to our joy, happiness, wealth, and good success. *"Therefore, whether you eat or drink, or whatever you do, do all to the glory of God."* 1 Corinthians 10:31.

BUILDING BLOCK 10

Balance

Have you ever felt wishy-washy? Are you constantly confused? Are you tired of asking questions and not getting the correct answers? Are you hanging on by a thread? Are you absolutely burned out? Well, it is time to activate the *Law of Balance*.

The *Law of Balance* is a Spiritual Principle reminding us of the importance of maintaining equilibrium with the Mind, Body, Soul, and Spirit. We must also understand that everything has an opposite and complementary force. For example, day and night, hot and cold, joy and sorrow, desire and disgust, and so on. Beyond a shadow of a doubt, it applies to our thoughts, emotions, actions, reactions, and beliefs.

When we are in balance, we experience harmony, peace, joy, and contentment. On the other hand, we experience stress, conflict, and dissatisfaction when out of balance. Why would this happen to us? It is a part of the Cycle and Vicissitudes of Life, and no one is exempt. Is this Biblical?

Absolutely. *"To everything there is a season, A time for every purpose under heaven: A time to be born, And a time to die; A time to plant, And a time to pluck what is planted."* Ecclesiastes 3:1-2.

In finding the optimal point between two extremes or opposing forces, the *Law of Balance* teaches us how to achieve harmony, peace, joy, and contentment among the four aspects of our being: the Mind, the Body, the Soul, and the Spirit. If we miss one aspect of this foundational equation, we allow the psyche to fill in the gaps of where we fall short, where we cannot stand tall, or what we do not understand. Why? It holds our secrets, weaknesses, traumas, lies, or whatever.

In the Realm of the Spirit, we must rightly divide what occurs within the Mind, Body, Soul, and Spirit. If not, an imbalance will occur from the inside out, appearing as negative thoughts, behaviors, habits, desires, words, actions, and reactions.

What is the big deal about these four aspects of our being? For example, when we have negative thinking or debauched internal chatting issues, we do not want to address the body; we must address the MIND. We do not want to address the mind if we catch a cold; we must address the BODY. We do not want to address the body when dealing with trauma; we must address the SOUL. When we need to repent or forgive, we do not want to address the mind; we must address the SPIRIT first. And then it may require us to deal with other areas, but we must know where to target our energy.

How do we rightly divide the Mind, Body, Soul, and Spirit, *As It Pleases God*? We must align ourselves with the Word of God. Here is what we must know: *"For the word of God is living and powerful, and sharper than any two-edged sword, piercing even to the division of soul and spirit, and of joints and marrow, and is a discerner of the thoughts and intents of the heart."* Hebrews 4:12. We can tiptoe around the Word of God all we like, but when it comes down to understanding our WHY, we need to know this, period! Once done, we must always stay on ready to:

- ☐ Identify an imbalance.
- ☐ Understand the imbalance, seed, root, or cause.
- ☐ Plan and take action to restore balance.
- ☐ Monitor progress.
- ☐ Repeat if necessary.

What if we choose not to use the *Law of Balance*? Imbalances will occur by default, appearing as longings, voids, lusts, thirsts, addictions, negative habits, rotten fruits, and flawed character traits. Furthermore, masks, lies, and cover-ups worsen our issues. Why? *"A false balance is an abomination to the Lord, But a just weight is His delight."* Proverbs 11:1.

Whatever balance we choose, be it false or just, it takes the same amount of energy; therefore, it behooves us to engage in beneficial balances. Listed below are a few ways to enhance the *Law of Balance*, but not limited to such:

- ☐ Be aware of your current state of being: balanced or imbalanced.
- ☐ Prioritize your time and energy by focusing on what is most important to you.
- ☐ Do not waste time on negativity.
- ☐ Set clear boundaries and read.

- ☐ Learn to kindly say 'no' to commitments that do not align with your values, goals, passions, or Divine Blueprint.
- ☐ Reduce exposure to stressful or toxic people, places, and things.
- ☐ Recharge your physical and mental well-being.
- ☐ Take breaks and sleep well.
- ☐ Engage in time management.
- ☐ Set limits on social media use.
- ☐ Set realistic goals.
- ☐ Break them down into manageable steps to avoid feeling overwhelmed.
- ☐ Learn to delegate tasks.
- ☐ Spend time in nature.
- ☐ Cultivate a positive mindset.
- ☐ Practice gratitude.
- ☐ Be proactive.
- ☐ Be encouraging and accountable.
- ☐ Document in your journal.
- ☐ Avoid self-criticism or negative self-talk.
- ☐ Practice forgiveness and repent often.
- ☐ Use mind maps to stay on track.
- ☐ Use the Fruits of the Spirit.
- ☐ Behave Christlike.

The *Law of Balance* is not a rat race or mad dash to the finish line. It is a step-by-step journey into our Divine Destiny or the unveiling of our Predestined Blueprint. When taking the journey, *As It Pleases God*, repeat this constantly: "*Your word is a lamp to my feet And a light to my path.*" Psalm 119:105. Why is this so important? "*For we walk by faith, not by sight.*" 2 Corinthians 5:7.

BUILDING BLOCK 11

Surrender

Does surrendering make you feel weak? Do you despise having to take the higher road? Do you dislike being submissive? Are you a people-pleaser? Are you tired of having to fix everything? Have you ever felt like you were struggling to achieve your goals, no matter how hard you tried? Have you ever felt frustrated, anxious, or overwhelmed by life's challenges and uncertainties? Then, my solemn word to you is, 'Surrender,' *As It Pleases God*.

The *Law of Surrender* is a Spiritual Principle of letting go of our need for control and accepting the things we cannot change. As life happens, it is difficult to let go without resistance or judgment, especially if we do not know what to do or how. Nor is it easy to trust the process of our Spiritual Journey when we have been abused, traumatized, rejected, or abandoned. There is always hope regardless of where we are or what we have been through; thus, we must surrender it, them, or that. The Bible says, *"Come to Me, all you who labor and are heavy laden, and I will give you rest. Take My yoke upon you and learn from Me, for I am gentle and lowly in heart, and you will find rest for your souls. For My yoke is easy and My burden is light."* Matthew 11:28-30.

If we place God at the forefront, *As It Pleases Him*, we can gain Spiritual Leverage and Favor with the *Law of Surrender*. Really? Yes, really. Romans 12:1 says, *"I beseech you therefore, brethren, by the mercies of God, that you present your bodies a living sacrifice, holy, acceptable to God, which is your reasonable service."*

Surrendering does not mean giving up, quitting, sitting around twiddling our thumbs, losing hope, or doing nothing. It means trusting that God knows what is best for us according to our Predestined Blueprint. When we submit and open ourselves to receive Divine Guidance, Inspiration, and Support from the Heavenly of Heavens, we can resist people, places, and things causing misalignment. Is this Biblical? I would have it no other way, *"Therefore submit to God. Resist the devil and he will flee from you."* James 4:7.

When we constantly resist people, places, and things without submitting first, we lose control by trying to maintain it. However, if we give control to God, *As It Pleases Him*, He gives us the power to overcome, endure, sustain, or maintain. Although it may not be Supernatural Power, it is enough power to get us through whatever with whomever.

How do we get to the Supernatural Power status? First, we must invoke and align with the Holy Trinity (The Father, Son, and Holy Spirit). Secondly, by allowing ourselves to flow with our Divinely Ordained Rhythm rather than against it, we enable the Blood of Jesus to cover us as it should and the Holy Spirit to guide, nudge, and protect us. Thirdly, we must master the Fruits of the Spirit and behave Christlike. And fourthly, we must be Spiritually Trained and Commissioned in our Blueprinted Purpose.

Remember, when dealing with the Supernatural from the Heavenly of Heavens, there are also Supernatural Responsibilities and Culpabilities. For this reason, the normal amount of power, grace, and mercy will suffice if we become a work-in-progress, *As It Pleases God*, using the Fruits of the Spirit and behaving Christlike. What can this do for us? We can still shake the boots off the enemy and break yokes, but at our capacity or Divine Blueprint, instead of taking on what we cannot Spiritually Handle or have not been Spiritually Trained to do. So, it behooves us to master the *Law of Surrender* before embarking upon the SUPER anything.

For the record, there is nothing weak about the *Law of Surrender*; it is a profound display of strength, ensuring we think before speaking, doing, or becoming. I consider this a Spiritual Pause to control our negative impulses or tendencies, allowing us to test the Spirit, ask questions, get an understanding, or glean wisdom. If we approach this Divine Principle correctly, and *As It Pleases God*, we can tap into our intuition, creativity, and internal reservoir of Divine Wisdom.

In *Building Our Own Table*, God wants us to get into a building block mindset, allowing one positive characteristic to build another, *As It Pleases Him*. For example, *"But also for this very reason, giving all diligence, add to your faith virtue, to virtue knowledge, to knowledge self-control, to self-control perseverance, to perseverance godliness, to godliness brotherly kindness, and to brotherly kindness love."* 2 Peter 1:5-7. When stacking Spiritual Building Blocks in such a manner, the *Law of Surrender* becomes easier to do. Why? According to the Heavenly of

Heavens, there are positive and fruitful benefits associated with Spiritually Stacking for the greater good.

How do we surrender to God, *As It Pleases Him*? We are all different, and He may require more or less from us depending on our Predestined Blueprint. For this reason, it is best to develop a *Spirit to Spirit* Relationship with Him to download specific or encrypted details from the GIVER to the intended receiver. What does this mean? No one can access our Divine Blueprinted Details outside of the Holy Trinity and the Divine Recipient.

Although some go to the dark side to get glimpses of our Divine Blueprint, they cannot see all the details. For example, we know there is a Garden of Eden with an approximation of its location, yet we do not have the exact details. Why? It is hidden within each of us. If we check our DNA structure, it is hidden in plain sight, yet VEILED to the owner of their Spiritual Portion. It is one of the reasons we must Spiritually Till, Surrender, and Align with our own ground without passing the buck.

In light of this, we cannot lay the blame elsewhere if we leave this information on the table without gaining access to what rightly belongs to us. Nevertheless, listed below are the Spiritual Basics to keep us in correct standing with God, but not limited to such:

- ☐ **Willingness.** You must become a WILLING VESSEL, surrendering to God's Divine Will, *As It Pleases Him*, with a confessing and repenting heart. *"If we confess our sins, He is faithful and just to forgive us our sins and to cleanse us from all unrighteousness."* 1 John 1:9.

- ☐ **Prayer.** You must spend time in prayer, asking God to guide, provide, teach, protect, and prepare you on your Spiritual Journey. Repeat continuously: *"I can do all things through Christ who strengthens me."* Philippians 4:13.

- ☐ **Gratitude.** You must exhibit gratefulness for the good, bad, or indifferent. Gratefulness helps remove the tendency to complain, bicker, fuss, and fight against the Will of God. In addition, it aids in creating a win-win out of a seemingly bad situation. *"Enter into His gates with thanksgiving, And into His courts with praise. Be thankful to Him, and bless His name."* Psalm 100:4.

- ☐ **Trust.** You must trust in God's Plan, knowing that everything happens for a reason with a lesson, testing, or Blessing attached. Read this daily: *"Trust in the Lord with all your heart, And lean not on your own understanding; In all your ways acknowledge Him, And He shall direct your paths."* Proverbs 3:5-6.

- ☐ **Letting go.** You must let go of the desire to control everything, allowing God to do what He does best. This release includes fears, doubts, traumas, unforgiveness, unbelief, and so on. Anything negative has to go, period. Then repeat: *"Not my will, but Yours, be done."* Luke 22:42.

- ☐ **Humility.** God loves a humble Spirit, and it allows Divine Favor to attach itself to you. *"But He gives more grace. Therefore He says: "God resists the proud, But gives grace to the humble."* James 4:6.

- ☐ **Patience.** You must be patient. However, when in a waiting period, you must prepare, plan, learn, and become proactive while waiting for God's Divine Timing. *"And let us not grow weary while doing good, for in due season we shall reap if we do not lose heart."* Galatians 6:9.

Once done, in our *Spirit to Spirit* alone time with our Heavenly Father, along with our Spiritual Journal in hand, ask questions and document the answers instead of begging. What if we get nothing? Document that too; the answer may come later or have already been documented. Here are a few ways to a Spiritual Approach in our *Spirit to Spirit* alone time, *As It Pleases God*, but not limited to such:

- ☐ I surrender this situation to my Heavenly Father.
- ☐ I trust that everything will work out for my good.
- ☐ How did I get here?
- ☐ Where did I go wrong?
- ☐ What do You want me to do in this situation?
- ☐ What do I need to learn?
- ☐ Why must I learn this?
- ☐ What is the next best step?
- ☐ How can this benefit the Kingdom and others?
- ☐ Please show me the way.
- ☐ Proactively give thanks and again when answered.

In this *Spirit to Spirit* session of surrender, here are a few things to avoid:

- ☐ Negativity.
- ☐ Criticizing.
- ☐ Complaining.
- ☐ Blaming.
- ☐ Wallowing.
- ☐ Lying.
- ☐ Levying curses.
- ☐ Player hating.
- ☐ Spirit of Disobedience.
- ☐ Greed.
- ☐ Pompousness.

Why can we not come into the Presence of God just as we are? Due to having free will, we can come as we please. Nevertheless, when doing so, we must exhibit RESPECT when in His Divine Presence. There are Spiritual Rules to the GAME of LIFE; if we do not know them, it is time to get in the know.

Even if we fall short in some areas, it does not mean we should lose respect for ourselves, others, or God Almighty. He loves us all, regardless of our idiosyncrasies; therefore, our responsibility is to activate the *Law of Surrender*, run our own race, and lend a helping hand to the next man. As Philippians 4:6-7 says, *"Be anxious for nothing, but in everything by prayer and supplication, with thanksgiving, let your requests be made known to God; and the peace of God, which surpasses all understanding, will guard your hearts and minds through Christ Jesus."*

www.DrYBur.com

BUILDING BLOCK 12
Reflection

Have you ever seen your reflection without having a reflector? Can you see who you really are? How do you see yourself? How do others see you? When the mirror is turned on us, what will we see?

The *Law of Reflection* is a Spiritual Principle describing how light behaves when it encounters a reflective surface and a means of measuring or viewing ourselves. This process applies to all types of reflective surfaces, including mirrors, glass, water, or optical systems, describing how light rays reflect off a surface or lead into all things Spiritual, such as Spiritual Illumination, Enlightenment, or Lamps. What does Spirituality have to do with anything? *"As in water face reflects face, So a man's heart reveals the man."* Proverbs 27:19.

Whatever we experience in our external reality reflects our internal state of being, even if we are in denial. We often call this self-reflecting, knowing nothing about the Spiritual Laws surrounding it, which is also linked to the *Law of Cause and Effect.* We will deal with the other side of this with the next Building Block. So, let us go deeper...

Unbeknown to most, a worldly mirror shows us what we are thinking, saying, feeling, believing, and experiencing through our actions, reactions, words, behaviors, demeanor, fruits, character, or the lack thereof. All of these determine if we become a deflector or reflector in the Eye of God.

With the *Law of Reflection*, we positively or negatively attract or repel people, places, things, situations, and events based upon our Spiritual Mirror. To transform ourselves, *As It Pleases God*, we must begin from the inside out, not from the outside in, getting rid of the negative junk, sludge, and debris spoiling our Spiritual Fruits and Christlike Character.

Why do we need to cleanse ourselves from the inside out? It becomes challenging to usher in the new when the old blocks it. Then again, when dealing with rotten fruits, the whole bunch will spoil, especially if we do not remove the rotten ones. However, there is a catch-22 in this matter...we must do a self-analysis or self-reflect, *As It Pleases God*, to determine what is rotten and what is good.

The bottom line is that we function better using the Fruits of the Spirit and behaving Christlike in or out of the Kingdom of God. If we use them, we will improve by default, regardless of whether we are Believers. Blasphemy, right? Wrong. "*But the fruit of the Spirit is love, joy, peace, longsuffering, kindness, goodness, faithfulness, gentleness, self-control. Against such there is no law.*" Galatians 5:22-23. The Fruits of the Spirit are a Free-For-All.

More importantly, the Fruits of the Spirit provide humanity with the best Spiritual Mirror or self-reflection. How is this possible, especially when developing our people skills? Developing skills on any level does not mean they are of Spiritual Quality, *As It Pleases God*. We can develop ourselves until we are blue in the face. When dealing with the *Law of Reflection*, it does not mean it is Christlike or up to Kingdom Quality, Standards, or Poshness. Why? *"Every way of a man is right in his own eyes, But the Lord weighs the hearts."* Proverbs 21:2.

According to the Heavenly of Heavens, use the Fruits of the Spirit when in doubt about anything or anyone. Why? With any type of self-reflection, we cannot go wrong using Love, Joy, Peace, Patience, Kindness, Goodness, Faithfulness, Gentleness, and Self-Control. In using them, everything that is good, bad, or indifferent must provide a stepping stone, a lesson, or an understanding. If we DO NOT know this Divine Principle, we cannot Spiritually Enforce it or demand it to Spiritually Yield.

What if we decline to use our Spiritual Mirror? Without using the *Law of Reflection*, we become subjected to life-reflection thieves and mangled fruits. According to the Word of God: *"The thief does not come except to steal, and to kill, and to destroy. I have come that they may have life, and that they may have it more abundantly."* John 10:10.

How does a thief get in? Through unresolved envy, jealousy, pride, greed, pompousness, coveting, and competitiveness. Be it within us or them, they get in! Nonetheless, we are responsible for pulling out our Spiritual Mirror, getting it, them, or that out of our lives.

Listed below are a few ways to engage in the *Law of Reflection*, but not limited to such:

- ☐ Develop a *Spirit to Spirit* Connection with God.
- ☐ Keep a journal.
- ☐ Document your thoughts and emotions.

- ☐ Understand why you feel a certain way.
- ☐ Repent and forgive yourself or others.
- ☐ Meditate, reflect, or calm your mind.
- ☐ Focus on what you are doing without distractions.
- ☐ Spend time in nature.
- ☐ Listen to music or read a book.
- ☐ Exercise to release tension.
- ☐ Seek feedback.
- ☐ Practice gratitude.
- ☐ Understand your strengths and weaknesses.
- ☐ Engage in creative activities.
- ☐ Get therapy, a mentor, or counseling.
- ☐ Share.

Can self-reflection really work for us? Absolutely! *"But let a man examine himself, and so let him eat of the bread and drink of the cup."* 1 Corinthians 11:28. By working on ourselves, *As It Pleases God*, with a work-in-progress mentality, He will help us along the way. The key is to TRY!

What guarantee do we have for putting in the effort? The Breath of Life is our guarantee! Therefore, *"Examine yourselves as to whether you are in the faith. Test yourselves. Do you not know yourselves, that Jesus Christ is in you?—unless indeed you are disqualified."* 2 Corinthians 13:5. If one does not feel this is a guarantee, try living without the Breath of Life, or when fighting for every breath!

Better yet, come back and talk to me when you need what money cannot buy; you will sing a different tune. Nevertheless, do not let it get to this point: *"Let us search out and examine our ways, and turn back to the Lord."* Lamentations 3:40.

BUILDING BLOCK 13

Cause and Effect

Why are you doing what you do? Why are you NOT doing what you should? Do you know what you should or should not do? Do you care? The *Law of Cause and Effect* is the most well-known Spiritual Principle and is often overlooked, misused, and abused.

We are accustomed to the external *Law of Cause and Effect*, forgetting about the internal seeds, roots, and fruits. In addition, this Spiritual Law is also intertwined and hidden in the *Law of Seedtime and Harvest*.

Although both Spiritual Laws are technically the same, they are broken down differently, dealing with regrafting before an external harvest and internal cause and effect.

Unfortunately, regardless of which side of the totem pole we are on, our internal issues are causing our external effects. If we do not approach the *Law of Cause and Effect* this way, it will turn our lives upside down while thinking we have it going on.

What is the big deal? The blaming game associated with the effects is a big deal. If we proactively account for the cost of the cause, we would most often divert the effects. What does this mean? If we understood the impact of what we are doing beforehand, we would change our approach. Really? Yes, really!

Whatever we see or do not see, everything is energy vibrating at different frequencies, such as low, medium, high, or supernaturally. How is this possible, especially when we cannot see, feel, or hear vibrations? Unfortunately, this is where Spiritual Deception, Omission, and Erring come into play, causing us to 'get got' with our lack of understanding.

We have the same Spiritual Powers and Frequencies Adam and Eve possessed in the Garden of Eden to communicate with our Heavenly Father. They are only hidden under something else, which must be Spiritually Tilled and Cultivated, *As It Pleases God*. If not, it remains hidden, as we operate in an internal deficit instead of the fullness therein.

Here is the deal: Once again, we are Spiritual Beings, having a human experience regardless of our ability to see, hear, touch, taste, or smell tangibly or intangibly. What does this mean? First, our tangible experiences and senses are connected to our earthly being. Secondly, our intangible senses are vibrational and connected to our Spiritual Being. The same way we see, hear, touch, taste, or smell physically, we can do in the Spiritual. How? Once again, everything is energy.

We emit vibrations through our thoughts, emotions, words, and actions. If they are not released, reading our vibrational efforts will become harder to dissect unless we are Spiritually Trained. How? Our vibrations create a magnetic field around us that attracts, reflects, or repels other vibrations that match, clash, create static, or induce a shock. For example, when touching someone, there are times when we will experience a shock out of nowhere—it is all energy. It is nothing weird; we all have it. Some know and understand how to use it, and some do not.

In the *Law of Cause and Effect*, a Psychiatrist will read our actions, thoughts, beliefs, words, and reactions to pinpoint our traumas, problems, or habits to determine a diagnosis or effects. A Spiritual Doctor from the Heavenly of Heavens will read vibrational energy first, then align actions, thoughts, beliefs, words, and reactions to pinpoint the seed, root, yoke, stronghold, or soul tie. Once the condition is determined, they will use a Spiritual Mirror and the *Law of Cause and Effect* of our traumas, problems, or habits to determine a Spiritual Diagnosis of our condition. While simultaneously aligning everything with Spiritual Laws and Principles to create wholeness and healing, *As It Pleases God*.

What is the difference between the two, especially when doing basically the same thing? One is based on learned information and understanding WITHOUT Spiritual Laws, Principles, Protocols, or the Word of God. The other is based on practical and learned knowledge of psychotherapy, along with Spiritual Laws, Principles, Protocols, Understanding, and the Word of God.

Regardless of our choices, we should not leave God out of our equational efforts when dealing with the *Law of Cause and Effect*. Why? First, we are created in the Image of God. Secondly, we must become AWARE of where and why we are falling short. Thirdly, we must know and understand the areas where we must STAND TALL in the Eye of God. For this reason, I have two Spiritual Seals in this matter:

- ☐ **Seal One**: James 1:23-24 says, *"For if anyone is a hearer of the word and not a doer, he is like a man observing his natural face in a mirror; for he observes himself, goes away, and immediately forgets what kind of man he was."*

- ☐ **Seal Two**: Psalm 127:1 says, *"Unless the Lord builds the house, They labor in vain who build it; Unless the Lord guards the city, The watchman stays awake in vain."*

BUILDING BLOCK 14

Non-judgment

In the *Law of Non-Judgment*, it is crucial to avoid judging yourself and others. Instead, practice compassion and understanding, gleaning the information, lesson, understanding, curiosity, or anything associated with it positively. Why? Beyond measure, judging creates separation, conflict, rejection, and suffering, while accepting creates connection, harmony, love, and peace.

Although we do not talk about this Spiritual Law much, it is profound in our growth process, *As It Pleases God*. When using a Spiritual Tool of Learning for ourselves, the goal is to become better, stronger, and wiser for the greater good, not to degrade, downplay, or lie to ourselves. *"Nor give place to the devil."* Ephesians 4:27.

For the record, the *Law of Non-Judgment* does not mean we condone or agree with everything. However, we are responsible for recognizing the potential of every being, good, bad, or indifferent, while learning, growing, and sowing back into the Kingdom of God using the Fruits of the

Spirit. Why is this so important in the Eye of God? It frees us from guilt, shame, resentment, anger, or any negative attachments associated, allowing us to live with more joy, love, and gratitude.

More importantly, we never know a man's story until we walk in his shoes. Plus, we never want the issues we have judged to find their way to our back door. How does it find its way to our back door? Frankly, if we pass negative judgment, we do so by sensibly guarding our front door (home or family life). When we are so busy judging and guarding people, places, and things in our own strength to protect the home front or an image, we leave the back door unguarded. Is this Biblical? Absolutely! *"Judge not, that you be not judged. For with what judgment you judge, you will be judged; and with the measure you use, it will be measured back to you."* Matthew 7:1-2.

The *Law of Non-Judgment* helps us to remain Spiritually Sober. Why? We all have issues, we all have something to work on, and we all are a work-in-progress. Unfortunately, we are left to our own devices if we do not involve God in our sobriety. For this reason, the enemy will always look for an open door to bring shame to our names or discredit us. Really? Yes, really! Therefore, *"Be sober, be vigilant; because your adversary the devil walks about like a roaring lion, seeking whom he may devour."* 1 Peter 5:8.

What can we do to become better, stronger, and wiser, *As It Pleases God*? Walk in the Spirit! *"I say then: Walk in the Spirit, and you shall not fulfill the lust of the flesh. For the flesh lusts against the Spirit, and the Spirit against the flesh; and these are contrary to one another, so that you do not do the things that you wish."* Galatians 5:16-17.

The *Law of Non-Judgment* is a Spiritual Principle that can significantly impact our lives. Here are a few examples of how this law can be applied:

- [ ] You can start by becoming aware of your thoughts and language when discussing others or situations. *"Keep your heart with all diligence, For out of it spring the issues of life."* Proverbs 4:23.

- [ ] Refrain from using negative or judgmental language and approach things open-mindedly. *"Death and life are in the power of the tongue, And those who love it will eat its fruit."* Proverbs 18:21.

- [ ] Practice empathy and put yourself in other people's shoes before making assumptions or judgments about them. *"Let no corrupt word proceed out of your mouth, but what is good for necessary edification, that it may impart grace to the hearers."* Ephesians 4:29.

- [ ] Instead of judging others for their actions or beliefs, try to understand their origin and the WHY, showing empathy. This approach can help to build stronger relationships and create a more positive environment. *"If anyone among you thinks he is religious, and does not bridle his tongue but deceives his own heart, this one's religion is useless."* James 1:26.

- [ ] Avoid making assumptions about people based on appearance, race, gender, or other characteristics. Everyone is unique and deserving of respect and consideration. "*Let your speech always be with grace, seasoned with salt, that you may know how you ought to answer each one.*" Colossians 4:6.

☐ Focus on your own actions and behaviors rather than criticizing or judging others. By being the best version of yourself, you can inspire others to do the same. "*Even a fool is counted wise when he holds his peace; When he shuts his lips, he is considered perceptive.*" Proverbs 17:28.

☐ Do not intentionally bring harm to anyone. "*Therefore, let us not judge one another anymore, but rather resolve this, not to put a stumbling block or a cause to fall in our brother's way.*" Romans 14:13.

Remember, the goal is to cultivate a non-judgmental attitude that promotes understanding and compassion. The *Law of Non-Judgment* is about acceptance, kindness, and compassion. We can create a more harmonious and peaceful world by embracing this Spiritual Principle, *As It Pleases God.*

BUILDING BLOCK 15

Manifestation

What are you hoping for? Do you know what you are manifesting? Do you know why you are manifesting? Is manifesting working for you? Are you aware of the Spiritual Principles behind the *Law of Manifestation*? Are you putting the *Law of Manifestation* into its proper perspective?

The *Law of Manifestation* is a powerful concept that can profoundly impact your life, the lives of others, and the Kingdom of God. Simply put, your thoughts, desires, words, actions, reactions, and beliefs create your reality. If you focus on the positive, you will attract positive experiences. Conversely, if you focus on the negative, you will attract negative experiences. Even though you are subjected to both, whatever you focus on, think about, speak of, or believe in, positively or negatively, you will attract into your life. Why? Everything is energy! Like attracts like, and the unlike is the lesson.

How does the *Law of Manifestation* work? Manifestation refers to the process of turning an idea, thought, belief, or desire into a tangible reality. According to the Heavenly of Heavens, it is also a gleaning, planning, and preparing process for our Predestined Blueprint. When we properly govern our thoughts, emotions, reactions, actions, and desires, *As It Pleases God*, it activates our manifestation process, bringing forth favor, provisions, and instructions.

Some people believe that manifestation can be enhanced by using tools such as affirmations, visualization techniques, and meditation, which is a half-truth. Why? First, we are adaptable, trainable, and impressionable, learning anything with time. And just because we have mastered whatever with whomever does not mean it is suitable for us or beneficial.

Secondly, without the Holy Trinity, we are limited to goal-setting and personal development without the Divine Blueprint. Therefore, when using the *Law of Manifestation*, it is only wise to manifest what Spiritually Aligns with us, *As It Pleases God*, instead of playing Russian Roulette, jumping from one thing or one person to the next. Why? We must ABIDE. *"If you abide in Me, and My words abide in you, you will ask what you desire, and it shall be done for you."* John 15:7.

Abiding is often associated with a sense of stability, steadfastness, and commitment. Meanwhile, abiding in the Oneness of God incorporates remaining faithful and obedient to the Word of God with a state of inner peace or serenity. This state of being is where one can remain calm and centered even in the face of challenges or difficulties, creating a win-win out of a seemingly lose-lose situation, circumstance, or event. *"Knowing all things work together for good to those who love God, to those who are the called according to His purpose."* Romans 8:28.

Thirdly, if the motivations behind what we manifest are unjust, doubtful, or debaucherous, our manifesting efforts will turn against us, or we will outright turn on ourselves. Why is this so important? According to the Bible, it says: *"But let him ask in faith, with no doubting, for he who doubts is like a wave of the sea driven and tossed by the wind."* James 1:6. The word DOUBT puts a damper on our agenda when Spiritually Manifesting, particularly when we do not reverse it. Let us go deeper...

In the Eye of God, doubt represents the feeling of uncertainty, lack of conviction, or the absence of understanding about something or someone. More importantly, we will all feel this occasionally, especially when we avoid using the Fruits of the Spirit. How? For example, when we are unsure about a decision, skeptical of a claim, uncertain about our own abilities, or when we have received red flags, the feeling of doubt can activate our Spiritual Discernment or Compass, provoking prayer, repentance, forgiveness, or gratefulness. Doubt can be a normal and healthy part of our Spiritual Journey, as it allows us to question without making assumptions and consider new perspectives. In contrast, doubting God, our Divine Blueprint, the Blood of Jesus, or the Presence of the Holy Spirit is not normal!

In making this make sense, excessive or persistent doubt leads to stress, anxiety, wavering mindset, negative mental chatter, and indecisiveness, opening the door to negative attributes and character traits, such as fear, resentment, anger, hatefulness, jealousy, envy, pride, greed, coveting, and competitiveness. All of which can work against us when activating the *Law of Manifestation*. Why? Negativity, debauchery, or ill will must be canceled and repented before manifesting. If not, it will stir it, that, or them into the pot of what we are cooking up. As a result, we get a melting pot instead of a VESSEL of Greatness.

We need prayer, repentance, forgiveness, insight, foresight, and the Fruits of the Spirit to UNVEIL the best version of ourselves. If not, insecurity will attach itself to our manifesting efforts. Really? Yes, really! Please allow me to Spiritually Align: *"Now this is the confidence that we have in Him, that if we ask anything according to His will, He hears us. And if we know that He hears us, whatever we ask, we know that we have the petitions that we have asked of Him."* 1 John 5:14-15.

The key to harnessing the *Law of Manifestation* is to become mindful of your thoughts, words, and beliefs. If you catch yourself thinking or speaking negatively, take a moment to reframe them positively. For example, instead of thinking, 'I will never be able to accomplish my goals,' repeat consistently, *"I can do all things through Christ who strengthens me."* Philippians 4:13. We can achieve anything with the help of Christ Jesus. Matthew 21:22 says, *"And whatever things you ask in prayer, believing, you will receive."*

The *Law of Manifestation* is not about sitting back, twiddling your thumbs, and waiting for good things to fall into your lap. This Spiritual Law is about becoming Spiritually Proactive, TILLING your own ground, and doing your due diligence. Matthew 7:7 says, *"Ask, and it will be given to you; seek, and you will find; knock, and it will be opened to you."* The action is to ask, seek, and knock, NOT sit and seek or sit and envision!

Is visualization and manifesting the same? They are similar, but slightly different. Visualization is envisioning or creating mental pictures as if they are already in reality, requiring no action outside of faith, believing, and hoping. *"(As it is written, I have made thee a father of many nations,) before him whom he believed, even God, who quickeneth the dead, and calleth those things which be not as though they were."* Romans 4:17.

On the other hand, manifestation is putting in the ACTION to facilitate what we envision, desire, hope for, or believe. Our manifesting power will depend on our level of clarity, type of intention, the strength of our belief system, the level of our energetic vibration, and the alignment of our actions.

Why is this Spiritual Law so important when manifesting? *"Where there is no vision, the people perish: but he that keepeth the law, happy is he."* Proverbs 29:18. When using the *Law of Manifesting*, listed below are a few tips, but not limited to such:

- ☐ Know WHAT you want and WHY you want it.
- ☐ Be specific about what you want, and write it down in the present tense. *"Write the vision and make it plain on tablets, that he may run who reads it."* Habakkuk 2:2.
- ☐ Communicate with God through prayer, fasting for clarity, and asking for confirmation or guidance.
- ☐ Study the Bible, searching for verses about your situation, goal, or desire.
- ☐ Feel the emotions of having what you want.
- ☐ Express sincere gratitude.
- ☐ Release any doubts, fears, unforgiveness, or limiting beliefs blocking your manifestation efforts.
- ☐ Take time to create a mind map or road map.
- ☐ Continue to learn everything about what you are envisioning.
- ☐ Trust God's Divine Timing.
- ☐ Remain open to receiving with joy (from within) and happiness (externally).

- You can ask questions, but DO NOT complain, fuss, fight, or beg.
- Make sure it aligns with your true self, your Divine Purpose, and the highest and greatest good.

Remember, God is the Creator, and you are the co-creator; therefore, you must put everything into their proper perspective. As a co-creator, you have the power and responsibility to shape your reality with your uniqueness according to your Predestined Blueprint. More importantly, you must also RESPECT the free will and choices of others, as they are also co-creators of their own Spiritual Blueprint.

How do we know if we are on the right track? God will send us confirmation. Although it may vary in how He sends the confirmation, here are a few examples:

- Pay attention to open and closed doors with the nudging of the Holy Spirit through your conscience. Every open or closed door is not God Almighty; therefore, you must know the difference.
- You may see words or pictures relating to your desire.
- You encounter people, situations, or opportunities that support your goal.
- You feel a sense of peace.
- You feel positive and confident about what you are manifesting.
- You may experience coincidences, bringing you closer to your desire.
- You have vivid dreams or visions of what you desire or envision, which may offer insight and confirmation.

☐ You may receive a Testimony aligning with what you desire or envision.

"Now faith is the substance of things hoped for, the evidence of things not seen." Hebrews 11:1. With the *Law of Manifestation*, you have the power to create your reality. By rising above, focusing on positive thoughts, and taking inspired actions, *As It Pleases God*, you can manifest the life of your dreams.

BUILDING BLOCK 16

Transcendence

Are you too comfortable? Are you afraid to get out of your comfort zone? God sees you as GREAT; how do you see yourself? Better yet, how do you treat yourself? Do self-imposed limitations limit you? Are you ready to rise above whatever, with whomever? If your answer is 'yes,' let us transcend to the next level, *As It Pleases God*.

The *Law of Transcendence* is a powerful Spiritual Principle of elevation in or out of the Kingdom of God. The rise of our Mental, Physical, Emotional, and Spiritual developmental status is ideal in the Eye of God. Why? He has given everyone something to work with, leaving no man unable to grow and become better, stronger, and wiser. For this reason, we can rise above our limitations and reach new levels of understanding and growth, *As It Pleases Him*, not ourselves.

The *Law of Transcendence* encourages us to push ourselves beyond our comfort or limitation zones, embracing new challenges to achieve our full potential. If someone settles for half of their potential, I have no qualms with that; however, if they do, they have no reason to complain, fuss, fight, or become pessimistic about what they chose not to do. Why such sternness? It takes the same amount of energy to TRY to become better, stronger, and wiser as it would to opt for the cycle of déjà vu. It is all in the MINDSET! When dealing with *The WHY Blueprint*, we must become a WILLING work-in-progress and creatively-in-progress.

By embracing the *Law of Transcendence*, we can tap into our inner strength to rise above our current state of being and move beyond our self-imposed limitations. What if our limitations are not self-imposed? If they are not self-imposed, it is our responsibility to repose them. What does this mean? We should be at peace with them, allowing our strengths to supersede them. Why? We all have strengths and weaknesses; therefore, we should never allow a weakness to stop us or become haughty to cover it up; it could be our BLESSING in disguise.

From experience, every weakness, disability, or idiosyncrasy was a diamond in the rough for me, with a Spiritual Platform attached. Without all of them, *The WHY Blueprint*, Dr. Y. Bur, or my books would not exist, helping others to help themselves. Regardless of the rejection, closed doors, being overlooked, being thrown under the bus, or having my ideas pilfered and capitalized on without me, I am ten toes deep in the Kingdom, doing what I am called to do, leaving no willing man behind. If one possesses a heart posture, *As It Pleases God*, then find a way around it, them, or that; if there is no way...then CREATE one by *Building Your Own Table*.

When using *Spiritual Building Blocks*, we must transcend beyond our ego and connect with our higher self to experience Spiritual Tilling, Growth, and Enlightenment, *As It Pleases God*. Why? Pompousness will cause Spiritual Blinders to form, closing our eyes to reality and preventing us from doing the right thing.

Beginning with the *Law of Transcendence* means forcing the ROCK of our weakness to yield, similar to how Moses made a rock yield water in Exodus 17:6. In doing so, *As It Pleases God*, we must also understand that we have Spiritual Conditions in the yielding process. First, it must fill a need for the greater good when faced with challenges and scarcity. Secondly, we must do without, weaning ourselves from anger, frustration, pride, greed, and duality. Listed below are a few ways of getting started, but not limited to such:

- ☐ Start by identifying the limitations, weaknesses, habits, and idiosyncrasies holding you back or taunting you.
- ☐ Document the WHY in your Spiritual Journal.
- ☐ Decide to reach your full potential.
- ☐ Develop your character, people skills, and fruits.
- ☐ Set goals for yourself, challenging your limitations.
- ☐ Step outside of your comfort zone, one step at a time.
- ☐ Focus on developing your inner strength and resilience with mind maps and road maps.
- ☐ Persevere through any obstacles that may arise.
- ☐ Remain committed to growth, understanding, and wisdom, gleaning lessons from everything.
- ☐ Be open to learning new things and exploring new perspectives.
- ☐ Surrender to your Predestined Blueprint. If you fight against it, it will fight back. For this reason, Jesus

said, "Nevertheless not my will, but Yours, be done." Luke 22:42. So, surrender!
- ☐ Never give up on your Spiritual Journey or Divine Blueprint; it will yield in due season. "And let us not grow weary while doing good, for in due season we shall reap if we do not lose heart." Galatians 6:9.

By following these steps and embracing the *Law of Transcendence*, you can overcome any challenge, creating a harmonious win-win for yourself, your Bloodline, and the Kingdom of God.

BUILDING BLOCK 17

Self-Love

Self-Love has become one of the most confusing human attributes known to humanity. On one hand, we are taught not to be selfish; on the other, we are taught to love ourselves. Which is it, right? In this *Spiritual Building Block*, we will learn the difference from God's Divine Perspective, *As It Pleases Him*.

We are often taught *Self-Love* for personal development, well-being, and mental health, often forgetting about the Spirituality of it all. Not involving the Love of God or the Fruits of the Spirit in our *Self-Love* will cause us to 'get-got' by the enemy's tricks. Why? The ideology of *Self-Love* can become narcissistic without the Fruits of the Spirit and neglecting to behave Christlike. Then again, if we are not careful about our pessimistic behaviors, thoughts, beliefs, desires, actions, reactions, biases, and conditioning, we can turn on ourselves without knowing it. Unfortunately, this will quickly cause *Self-Love* to become selfish, spoiling our fruits, putting a bad taste in the mouths of others, and causing us to get a side-eye from God Almighty.

The *Law of Self-Love* is an essential Spiritual Principle that causes us to walk on eggshells. Why would we walk on eggshells when we should love ourselves? Loving ourselves as it pleases us is different from loving ourselves *As It Pleases God*. What is the difference? One is loving with the Spirit of God, and the other is loving in the flesh. Unfortunately, we cannot double-dutch in this matter, or we will trip ourselves up. How? We are known by our Fruits according to Galatians 5:22-23.

With the Love of God, using the Fruits of the Spirit, Spiritual Mirrors, and behaving Christlike helps us maintain balance from the inside out, not from the outside in. Why should we love like this? There is no law against the Fruits of the Spirit. More importantly, love is the first Spiritual Fruit, indicating the importance of building a foundational *Building Block* for all the other fruits.

Without love, all of the other fruits become null and void. Really? Yes, really! The Holy Spirit and the Blood of Jesus will not uphold us in our wrongdoings; they are designed to bring us OUT of them, not to operate in them. If we do, we are operating under a different set of Spiritual Laws outside of the Godly ones, so beware!

Once we love, *As It Pleases God*, what can the other Spiritual Fruits do for us? Once love becomes our foundation, then joy and peace become the inner state of being for a person living in harmony with God and others. Long-suffering or patience becomes the ability to endure difficult circumstances without giving up, giving in, or throwing in the towel, especially when the going gets rough. Kindness and goodness help us treat ourselves and others righteously with outright integrity. Faithfulness assists in building our loyalty to God, ourselves, and others. Gentleness is how we handle others when no benefits are associated, especially when doing good deeds of helpfulness, exercising thoughtfulness, and engaging proactively without being harsh, hateful, or rude.

With the compilation of all of the other Spiritual Fruits, self-control is the ability to resist temptation, govern ourselves accordingly, exercise restraints, and use the Fruits of the Spirit when it is hard to do so. Additionally, in a state of self-control or wavering control, we can repent, forgive, and let go, freeing the Mind, Body, and Soul from yokes, soul ties, and bondages, with the ability to say 'no' and mean it. According to the Heavenly of Heavens, these qualities represent the ideal Christlike Character that God will move Heaven and Earth to save, protect, and provide for when using the *Law of Self-Love, As It Pleases Him*.

Meanwhile, with our love of ourselves, we operate with any type of debauched fruits, furthering our agenda. This feat is accomplished without a Spiritual Mirror reflecting our behaviors, thoughts, actions, and beliefs that require self-correcting. As a result, we behave however we desire to get what we want, when we want it, how we want it, and despite who it hurts, amid doing what we do, making the love of self our ultimate mission.

To add insult to injury, the love of self is happening while appearing right in our own eyes. What does this mean? We are Spiritually Blind, thinking we are seeing clearly. We are Spiritually Deaf, thinking we are hearing the Voice of God. We are Spiritually Mute, thinking we are speaking the Language of God from the Heavenly of Heavens, while spreading false propaganda contradicting the Fruits of the Spirit and Christlike Character. We are operating in dullness while thinking we are Spiritually Sharp. We are stiff-necked, feeling as if we are loose and fancy-free, swinging it high and low for the Kingdom and headed straight to the PIT. Is this really happening? Absolutely! For this reason, "*Let no one say when he is tempted, 'I am tempted by God'; for God cannot be tempted by evil, nor does He Himself tempt anyone.*" James 1:13.

Do we not have free will to do whatever we like with whomever? Absolutely! However, when using the *Law of Self Love*, we must fall under the Spiritual Law without thinking we are above it. The moment we think we are above it, it invokes the Cycles and Vicissitudes of Life to teach us what we have failed to learn. We may experience feelings of burnout, exhaustion, regret, and resentment. We may also struggle with low self-esteem and have difficulty maintaining healthy and respectful relationships. Amid our mishaps, what have we not learned? RESPECT!

If we partake of anything Spiritual, respect must be given; if not, we inadvertently turn on ourselves from the inside out. Is this Biblical? I would have it no other way. The *Law of Self-Love* has two Spiritual Seals:

- ☐ **First Seal**: "*Do you not know that you are the temple of God and that the Spirit of God dwells in you? If anyone defiles the temple of God, God will destroy him. For the temple of God is holy, which temple you are.*" 1 Corinthians 3:16-17.

- ☐ **Second Seal**: "*And what agreement has the temple of God with idols? For you are the temple of the living God. As God has said: 'I will dwell in them and walk among them. I will be their God, and they shall be My people.'* " 2 Corinthians 6:16.

Self-Love in the Eye of God is loving our Temple, *As It Pleases Him*. We are the dwelling place of God, and we should avoid any actions, reactions, thoughts, beliefs, demeanor, words, or whatever goes against His Divine Will or our Predestined Blueprint. Why? *"For all the law is fulfilled in one word, even in this: 'You shall love your neighbor as yourself.' "* Galatians 5:14. If we cannot love ourselves properly, we cannot love others as God intended with the Fruits of the Spirit, and our people skills will suck, becoming putrefied ointment.

Why would we become putrefied? Rotten fruits, foolery, or hostile behavior ruin the value of our character and reputation. Please allow me to Spiritually Align: *"Dead flies putrefy the perfumer's ointment, and cause it to give off a foul odor; so does a little folly to one respected for wisdom and honor."* Ecclesiastes 10:1.

The *Law of Self-Love* is not a one-and-done Spiritual Law; it requires constant awareness, astuteness, intention, and action. Since we are all unique with different issues, traumas, beliefs, conditioning, and biases, with varying needs, wants, and desires, there is no one-size-fits-all remedy. In the same way, we all have different fingerprints, footprints, mindprints, and eyeprints; the same applies to applying the *Law of Self-Love*. We must develop a *Spirit to Spirit* Relationship with our Heavenly Father to apply the Blood of Jesus correctly and adequately use the Holy Spirit to train, guide, filter, nurture, and provide.

When you practice *Self-Love* authentically and *As It Pleases God*, you are better equipped to give love to others and contribute positively to the world around you. However, here are a few suggestions to help you practice *Self-Love*, but not limited to such:

- ☐ Be mindful of your thoughts and feelings.
- ☐ Take note of your inner chatter or self-talk, ensuring it is positive, productive, and fruitful.
- ☐ Become aware of how you react to people, places, situations, circumstances, and events.
- ☐ Challenge any negative or limiting beliefs with positive affirmations.
- ☐ Understand your true worth and believe in your Divine Potential.
- ☐ Be compassionate towards yourself and others.
- ☐ Speak to yourself and others with kindness and respect.
- ☐ Forgive yourself and others for mistakes, learning from everything.
- ☐ Celebrate achievements and acknowledge your efforts.
- ☐ Do not compare yourself to others.
- ☐ Do not judge yourself harshly; you are a work-in-progress.
- ☐ Be authentically you.
- ☐ Honor your values and beliefs with integrity.
- ☐ Follow your intuition or conscience.
- ☐ Express your opinions and emotions honestly and respectfully.
- ☐ Do not hesitate to say 'no' or set boundaries when necessary.
- ☐ Do not try to please others or fit in at the expense of your happiness or integrity.
- ☐ Be caring and helpful toward yourself and others.
- ☐ Take care of your mental health by managing stress, practicing relaxation techniques, meditating, or journaling.

- ☐ Enjoy what you love, and engage in hobbies or activities that bring you joy, fulfillment, and peace.
- ☐ Do something creative, having fun with yourself.
- ☐ Be playful and adventurous to invoke laughter.
- ☐ Reward yourself for your hard work and accomplishments.
- ☐ Pamper yourself with a massage, a bath, a book, relaxing music, or a movie.
- ☐ Respect yourself. Do not allow others to take advantage of you or disrespect you. Kindly excuse yourself!
- ☐ Value your time, energy, money, and space.
- ☐ Surround yourself with people who love, support, inspire, and motivate you.

Regardless of whether you are between the love of self versus *Self-Love*, remember, as a Temple of God, you are unique, stunning, worthy, lovable, and most of all, you are enough. God created you GREAT; everything you need is already there, and do not allow anyone to convince you otherwise. With the Spiritual Lamp guiding your footsteps, simply do your due diligence, *As It Pleases God*, and keep it moving in the Spirit of Excellence.

BUILDING BLOCK 18
Responsibility

Are you a person of your word? Can people count on what you say? Can you be trusted to do the right thing? Do you deflect your responsibilities onto others? Do you make excuses for not doing what you should do? Are you dealing with the consequences of not taking responsibility for your actions? The *Law of Responsibility* wants to share Divine Wisdom with you about your responses, liabilities, and the lack thereof.

Our responses and the lack thereof mean something, even if we pretend, put on masks, downplay our reality, or think we are levitating above others. In the Eye of God, responsibility is what it is, and He pulls no punches about what He expects from us, even if we think we have it going on.

The *Law of Responsibility* is wrapped in counting the cost of what we do, say, become, or engage in. Really? Yes, really! *"For which of you, intending to build a tower, does not sit down first and count the cost, whether he has enough to finish it— lest, after he has laid the foundation, and is not able to finish, all who see it begin to mock him, saying, 'This man began to build and was not able to finish.'* " Luke 14:28-30.

The cost of our thoughts, actions, decisions, words, and behaviors is a liability, especially if they are NOT well governed or exude pompousness. From the south, where I am from, we have colloquialisms of relevance stating: 'It is not what you say, it is how you say it!' 'It is not what you do; it is how you do it!' 'It is not what you become, but how you become it.'

What is so special about these colloquialisms? They help us consider the cost of our decisions, words, and actions to avoid the negative consequences before committing to them. How does this work? For example:

- ☐ Think before we speak.
- ☐ Think before we do something.
- ☐ Think before we move.
- ☐ Think before we engage.
- ☐ Think before we commit to something or someone.
- ☐ Think before we spend.
- ☐ Think before we attempt to deliberately destroy someone.

Thinking takes only a fraction of a second, and it takes less than that to destroy our lives by avoiding it. If we do not put actions behind our thoughts, they remain thoughts that can be corrected, counteracted, or overruled. When we put action behind our thoughts, they become seeds, positive or negative. Remember, positive thoughts equate to positive seeds or assets; negative thoughts produce negative ones with plausible liabilities.

The *Law of Responsibility* is hidden mostly within our HOW and WHY. For example, we can easily change our HOW once we understand the WHY behind what we do, say, and become, or the lack thereof. Listed below are a few things to consider when taking action, but not limited to such:

- ☐ What are the potential consequences of this action?
- ☐ Is this action legal?
- ☐ Is this action ethical or necessary?
- ☐ Will this action harm me or others?
- ☐ Do I have all the information I need to make an informed decision?
- ☐ What are my motivations for taking this action?
- ☐ Have I considered all possible alternatives?
- ☐ Have I considered the opinions and perspectives of others?
- ☐ Will this action have long-term consequences?
- ☐ Will this action conflict with any of my values or beliefs?
- ☐ Have I considered the potential risks and benefits of this action?
- ☐ Am I willing to accept the consequences of this action?
- ☐ Will this action align with my goals, objectives, or Divine Blueprint?
- ☐ Is this action financially feasible?
- ☐ Will this action impact my health or well-being?
- ☐ Is this action consistent with my personal or professional image?
- ☐ Will this action make me happy or fulfilled?
- ☐ Is this action worth the time and effort required?
- ☐ Will this action bring me closer to my desired outcome or result?

- ☐ What does the Word of God say about this?
- ☐ Will the Fruits of the Spirit apply?
- ☐ Is it Christlike?

What if we do not have time to go over this list? I cannot manage or govern someone's time. Nevertheless, I must ask, 'How much time will we forfeit for not reviewing it?' If, for some reason, we are in a crunch for time, do the Fruits of the Spirit countdown:

1. Is it exhibiting **Love**?
2. Will it bring **Joy**?
3. Is it going to bring **Peace**?
4. Is it exhibiting **Patience**?
5. Is it displaying **Kindness**?
6. Is it revealing **Goodness**?
7. Is it showing **Faithfulness**?
8. Is it revealing **Gentleness**?
9. Is it demonstrating **Self-Control**?

Will this work? When *Building Our Own Table*, this 9-second countdown will not miss a beat! Not only is it a *Building Block*, but it is also a *Table Builder*. Says who? Says the Lord God Almighty: "*Unless the Lord builds the house, they labor in vain who build it; unless the Lord guards the city, the watchman stays awake in vain.*" Psalm 127:1.

The Fruits of the Spirit are like watchmen as we prepare and *Build Our Own Table*. Please allow me to Spiritually Align: "*Prepare the table, Set a watchman in the tower, Eat and drink. Arise, you princes, Anoint the shield! For thus has the Lord said to me: 'Go, set *a watchman, let him declare what he sees.'* " Isaiah 21:5-6. If one does not believe this, just use the *Law of Responsibility* with the Fruits of the Spirit for seven days and another seven days without them. The difference will revolutionize our lives as the 9-second countdown becomes a part of our Spiritual Approach.

Our Spiritual Approach is extremely crucial in the Eye of God. Why? Either we approach with Him involved, *As It Pleases Him*, or without Him, as it pleases ourselves. Remember, there is no law against using the Fruits of the Spirit; therefore, we should use them to our benefit, not our demise. Not taking responsibility can have negative consequences; *"For each one shall bear his own load."* Galatians 6:5. Here are a few adverse effects, but not limited to such:

- ☐ **Damaged relationships**: When trust is lost due to a lack of responsibility, people will cut their losses and move on.

- ☐ **Unreliability**: When people cannot rely on you, you are unwilling to admit fault or apologize; unfortunately, you become an eyesore or canker that will eventually be pruned.

- ☐ **Stunted growth**: By not taking responsibility for your actions, thoughts, behaviors, words, or reactions, you limit your ability to learn from your mistakes and grow. Without growth or willingness, you cannot change negative behaviors, habits, or patterns.

- **Increased stress and anxiety**: When you do not take responsibility for your actions, thoughts, behaviors, words, or reactions, you worry more about the consequences, try to shift blame, or play mind games, leading to increased stress, anxiety, and even guilt.

- **Legal and financial consequences**: Not taking responsibility for your actions, thoughts, behaviors, words, or reactions can have severe legal and financial consequences.

The willingness to admit, repent, correct our mistakes, and learn from our failures helps us avoid a negligent lifestyle as we grow, improve, achieve, and grow GREAT. *"So then each of us shall give account of himself to God."* Romans 14:12. When we take responsibility for our actions, we must:

- Learn from our mistakes while using the Word of God to Spiritually Align. *"For whatever things were written before were written for our learning, that we through the patience and comfort of the Scriptures might have hope."* Romans 15:4.

- Avoid repeating the same mistakes over and over by using the Holy Spirit. *"But the Helper, the Holy Spirit, whom the Father will send in My name, He will teach you all things, and bring to your remembrance all things that I said to you."* John 14:26.

- Seek feedback, improve our skills, and move toward our Predestined Blueprint, knowing everything will work itself out. *"And we know that all things work together for good to those who love God, to those who are the called according to His purpose."* Romans 8:28.

- [ ] Let go of the past. *"Brethren, I do not count myself to have apprehended; but one thing I do, forgetting those things which are behind and reaching forward to those things which are ahead, I press toward the goal for the prize of the upward call of God in Christ Jesus."* Philippians 3:13-14.

- [ ] Build trust and credibility with God, ourselves, and others. *"Let your light so shine before men, that they may see your good works and glorify your Father in Heaven."* Matthew 5:16.

- [ ] Align our actions, words, thoughts, beliefs, values, and principles to the Word of God. *"A wicked man hardens his face, But as for the upright, he establishes his way."* Proverbs 21:29.

- [ ] Enhance our self-esteem and confidence by walking uprightly, *As It Pleases God*. *"See then that you walk circumspectly, not as fools but as wise, redeeming the time, because the days are evil."* Ephesians 5:15-16.

- [ ] Exercise Integrity. *"The integrity of the upright will guide them, but the perversity of the unfaithful will destroy them."* Proverbs 11:3.

Remember, you cannot control others; you can only control your actions, reactions, thoughts, beliefs, words, and mindset. So, choose wisely and act responsibly, *As It Pleases God*, while moving forward in the Spirit of Excellence.

BUILDING BLOCK 19

Resonance

Are you equally yoked? Are you feeling soul-tied to someone else? Do you feel as if your equilibrium is off? Are you repelling or attracting the people, places, and things you desire?

The *Law of Resonance* is a forgotten Spiritual Principle that profoundly impacts our lives without us realizing it. The *Law of Resonance* states that objects or systems with similar frequencies, such as music, psychology, and Spirituality, tend to vibrate harmoniously. Simply put, we attract experiences and outcomes resonating with our thoughts, emotions, words, actions, and beliefs through the energy we emit. We often call it vibing, where we share thoughts, beliefs, ideas, behaviors, etc. Once again, similar to the *Law of Attraction*, like attracts like.

What is the difference between the *Law of Attraction* and *Resonance*? The *Law of Attraction* has a focal manifesting based upon the wants, needs, and desires of our WHY, and what we think or believe, positively or negatively. In contrast, the

Law of Resonance is the underlying Spiritual Law or *Building Block* supporting the *Law of Attraction* based on our frequency or energy.

If the quality of our *Attraction* is keeled, so is our *Resonance*. Why? They are intertwined. Simply put, the *Law of Resonance* explains why the *Law of Attraction* works or does not work in our favor. When they have mixed signals, we become confused, frustrated, and wavering, while becoming lukewarm, dull, and stiff-necked. Unfortunately, all of these are disdaining in the Eye of God. *"So then, because you are lukewarm, and neither cold nor hot, I will vomit you out of My mouth."* Revelation 3:16.

What is the big deal, especially when God loves us all? What we emit is not on God; it is on us! If one knows nothing about their frequency, they would be surprised at what they emit and attract. Rest assured that we are NOT on one accord with the Heavenly of Heavens. Really? Yes, really! God does not want us to be Spiritually Indifferent or Ineffective, half-heartedly doing things.

God wants us to fully commit to Him, the Kingdom, and our Divine Purpose. Why? Being lukewarm, disobedient, and dull makes us ineffective in our Spiritual Growth and our Spiritual Classroom, making us unprepared, unusable, and unequipped to deal with real Spiritual Matters.

For example, if we are vibing like the enemy, can we contend if we operate with the same negative energy? Can we fight fairly using the enemy's tactics? Unfortunately, we will be outsmarted because we lack understanding. How so? When dealing with energy, either we are equal or opposite! All else is a distraction. *"No one can serve two masters; for either he will hate the one and love the other, or else he will be loyal to the one and despise the other. You cannot serve God and mammon."* Matthew 6:24.

We must make a clear choice and commitment to serve God wholeheartedly without straddling the fence between two opposing forces. We cannot have one foot in the Kingdom of Heaven and one foot out of it, doing our own thing. If we do, confusion will become our portion. Before going any further, know this: *"For God is not the author of confusion but of peace, as in all the churches of the saints."* 1 Corinthians 14:33.

I am not here to pass judgment but to get us in Purpose on purpose according to our Predestined Blueprint. Therefore, our Spiritual Vibes must be on point and in queue (inline or alignment) to ensure we do not miss our Divine Cue (Spiritual Signal). Why? Open or hidden confusion will hinder our ability to hear from God and understand His Divine Will or Blueprint for our lives.

Although we trust in God, He has also set in motion Spiritual Laws we should know about. Failing to understand basic Spiritual Principles creates a disservice to ourselves and the Kingdom of God. Why? Everything is energy! Let us go a little deeper...

Energy is constantly vibrating at different frequencies. When two things vibrate at the same frequency, they are said to be in resonance with each other. What does this mean? A deeper level of understanding or compatibility between two or more people, places, and things. For example, activating the *Law of Resonance* with nature will help heal the weary psyche. Then again, connecting to the right people who Spiritual Align with us can help elevate us to the next level. Meanwhile, connecting with the wrong people will demote us Mentally, Physically, Emotionally,

Spiritually, and Financially. All in all, this Spiritual Law can work for us or against us.

Similarly, when we think positive thoughts and focus on positive outcomes, we resonate with positive energy, helping us attract more positive experiences. On the other hand, when we focus on negative thoughts and outcomes, we resonate with negative energy, attracting negative experiences. Although we will experience both, we should not waste precious time counteracting negative energy, especially when we can keep it positive straight out of the gate.

By understanding the *Law of Resonance* and learning to harness its power, we can create the life we truly desire. Whether through meditation, positive affirmations, visualization, the Word of God, the Fruits of the Spirit, or simply focusing on positive thoughts and outcomes, we can shift our energy and vibration to attract more of what we want and less of what we do not.

How do we shift from negative to positive energy? We can shift from negative to positive energy in many ways, but we must recognize what it is first. Negative energy can manifest in different ways, such as feelings of anxiety, stress, anger, fear, hatefulness, or sadness. It can also appear as physical symptoms such as headaches, fatigue, or muscle tension. Unbeknown to most, negative energy can be recognized by paying close attention to our thoughts, reactions, actions, emotions, physical sensations, and conscience.

Suppose we notice we are consistently experiencing negative feelings or awkward physical symptoms without a clear medical explanation. In this case, it may be a sign that we are carrying, manifesting, or harboring negative energy. Practicing gratitude, visualization, and positive affirmations while using the Word of God with the Fruits of the Spirit can shift or redirect negative energy.

The *Law of Resonance* is a fundamental force from the Heavenly of Heavens and cannot be blocked. Once again, we can shift energy and vibration to attract positive experiences and outcomes. Listed below are a few focal points of how to take action with this Spiritual Law, but not limited to such:

- ☐ Practice gratitude: List what we are grateful for in our Spiritual Journal daily.

- ☐ Get enough rest: Ensure we rejuvenate the Mind, Body, and Soul.

- ☐ Surround ourselves with positivity: Spend time with people who uplift, build, and nurture. If they bring us down, degrade us, or trigger trauma or drama, kindly plan an exit before the trauma becomes deeply rooted.

- ☐ Practice mindfulness: Be present in the moment and focus on the needful.

- ☐ Be kind and exhibit compassion: Help others and show empathy.

- ☐ Engage in laughing: As our Heavenly Medicine, laughter is excellent for reducing stress and boosting our moods. *"A merry heart does good, like medicine, but a broken spirit dries the bones."* Proverbs 17:22.

- ☐ Get outside: Spend time in nature and get fresh air and sunshine.

- ☐ Practice repentance and forgiveness: Let go of hatefulness, grudges, and revenge.

- ☐ Use positive and inspiring affirmations: Repeat them daily.

- ☐ Practice meditation: Reflective and grateful meditation is a great way to relax the mind, combat stress, and connect to God, *Spirit to Spirit*.

- ☐ Listen to enriching music: The power of music can powerfully affect our moods, thoughts, and feelings.

- ☐ Learn something new: Stimulate the mind by learning something new consistently with an understanding.

- ☐ Focus on solutions and the win-wins, not problems or the lose-lose: Instead of dwelling on problems, focus on finding solutions, *As It Pleases God*.

- ☐ Practice generosity: The *Law of Reciprocity* and Seedtime and Harvest are non-refutable. What we desire, give it! Put something in the pot, showing generosity without being on the take.

- ☐ Be open and properly guarded: Try new things and experiences with practical wisdom. It is often said, 'Nothing ventured, nothing gained.'

- ☐ Visualize: We should paint a mental picture, visualizing ourselves achieving our goals, desires, and Divine Mission. Mental conception has power; use it correctly, and it will reward us greatly.

Why is taking action so crucial in the Eye of God? Everything we see, hear, touch, taste, and smell is comprised of vibrating particles of energy. Unbeknown to most, our thoughts, words, actions, reactions, and emotions are energy, having their own frequency. Most of all, our beliefs, memories, habits, traumas, lusts, patterns, and conditioning have the ultimate vibrating forces, even if we hide their power or downplay their control.

Our subconscious programming is hidden within the psyche, reverberating what we feed our human faculties, similar to the sound of music coming from a speaker. The louder the volume, the more the speaker vibrates. The lower the volume, the less it vibrates. The key is to Spiritually Sync ourselves to Kingdomly Vibrations to ensure our receptors are not warped and we receive the correct signals. If not, interference prevents us from adequately seeing, hearing, speaking, understanding, and discerning, *As It Pleases God*. Unfortunately, this is when we call evil good and good evil.

When we think or feel something, we send out a wave of energy interacting with other waves, positively or negatively. Some are Spiritually Trained to read the energy, and some are not, depending on the frequency and intensity of our energy. Most would think this is superstitious or taboo, but it is not...we all possess this ability; we are just NOT AWARE of how to use it. Still, we are quick to negatively judge someone with this ability or brand them with stigmatizing labels, while at the same time wishing we possessed something we already have.

Now that you know the truth about how the *Law of Resonance* works, *As It Pleases God*, you can change your life for the greater good of all humanity.

www.DrYBur.com

BUILDING BLOCK 20
Service

Are you afraid to serve? Is it embarrassing to serve others? Do you enjoy being catered to? Can you give of yourself, expecting nothing in return? Are you making a positive impact on the lives of others?

According to the Heavenly of Heavens, we are designed to serve and be served. No one is exempt from this Spiritual Law for our Heaven on Earth Experience, even if we pretend we are or think the Bible is not fulfilling these Spiritual Laws from within us. For example, although we are Believers, it does not exempt us from the Spiritual Laws governing the earthly realm. For instance, no one is exempt from the Law of Gravity. The moment we think we are, we will become true believers of it once it is violated.

In this book, *Build Your Own Table*, no one is exempt from these Spiritual Laws. Once again, no one, and I mean no one, is exempt, even if we do not understand them, downplay them, or attempt to beat the system by playing Holy Holy as if we have God pegged. Although we have the Blood of Jesus to cover our sins as a form of Spiritual Atonement, it does not cover Spiritual Negligence.

Yes, the Blood of Jesus covers us so that we do not have to make those bloody animal sacrifices anymore, but it does not mean we do not need to exercise the Spiritual *Law of Repentance, Forgiveness, Love,* and so on. We need to REPENT! We need to FORGIVE! We need to LOVE each other! Someone stating otherwise is like telling us to place our hands on an open flame or play with fire, and we will NOT get burned. The Devil is a liar, and deception or the PIT is not our portion!

The ultimate FULFILLMENT of this relationship *Spirit to Spirit*, is the marriage of the Lamb (Jesus Christ) and his bride (the church) in the New Jerusalem. Until then, we have work to do!

When we do not understand the Blood of Jesus, we begin making up stuff on the fly to justify our folly as if Spiritual Laws are null and void. They are NOT null and void until the final Spiritual Seals are placed. What does this mean? All of the Servants of God have not been SEALED WITH A MARK; therefore, Divine Order is still RELEVANT. Blasphemy, right? Wrong. "*Then I saw another angel ascending from the east, having the seal of the living God. And he cried with a loud voice to the four angels to whom it was granted to harm the earth and the sea, saying, 'Do not harm the earth, the sea, or the trees till we have sealed the servants of our God on their foreheads.'* " Revelation 7:2-3.

Simply put, we must follow Divine Instructions, even if we do not understand, believe, or want to rebel. Why? Here is what we must know: "*So Samuel said: 'Has the Lord as great delight in burnt offerings and sacrifices, as in obeying the voice of the Lord? Behold, to obey is better than sacrifice, and to heed than the fat of rams.'* " 1 Samuel 15:22. If we have not been Spiritually Sealed or have obtained the Spiritual Mark on our foreheads, we have no reason to become rebellious, dull, or stiff-necked. How will we know when we receive the Sealed Mark? The same way we know we DO NOT have it!

The battle is between good and evil. The Spiritual Seal of the living God is placed on the foreheads of the righteous to protect them from hurt, harm, or danger. If we are a self-service station, we are going to run out of gas...Spiritual Gas, to be exact!

How can we avoid running out of gas? Feed God's sheep, *As It Pleases Him*, not as it pleases ourselves or to put on a show. Here is the deal: Regardless of what we believe or do not understand, do not mislead God's sheep, especially when unsure about something, knowing nothing about the Fruits of the Spirit or how to use them properly. Why? We become subjected to the other mark. What mark? The mark of the beast. Really? Yes, really! The nature of the beast will hang us out to dry, especially if we do not up the ante on Divine Wisdom, Spiritual Laws, and Heavenly Protocol.

How does the beast mark us? With fakeness and pretense. Why? Pretense zaps our joy with fleeting happiness, causing us to acquire the need to be served by those appearing less than us. Unfortunately, this causes us to get a temporary high or feeling of superiority. Meanwhile, behind closed doors, the invisible whip of insecurity becomes our self-induced cat-o'-nine-tails, causing the psyche to do a number on us.

What would cause the psyche to act in such a manner, especially when we are Believers? Once again, we are designed to serve and be served. It creates a double-edged sword if we opt out of serving only to be served, giving the beast leverage. Is this Biblical? I would have it no other way: *"Then a third angel followed them, saying with a loud voice, 'If anyone* worships the beast and his image, and receives his mark on his forehead or on his hand, he himself shall also drink of the wine of the wrath of God, which is poured out full strength into the cup of His indignation.'" Revelation 14:9-10.

What about the cat-o'-nine-tails on the psyche? *"And that servant who knew his master's will, and did not prepare himself or do according to his will, shall be beaten with many stripes. But he who did not know, yet committed things deserving of stripes, shall be beaten with few. For everyone to whom much is given, from him much will be required; and to whom much has been committed, of him they will ask the more."* Luke 12:47-48.

The *Law of Service* indeed determines the counterfeit mark or the Authentic Seal. Serving others, *As It Pleases God*, restores our internal joy apparatus, allowing happiness to last longer with more fulfillment without latching on to debilitating habits, vices, or lusts. Is this Biblical? Absolutely! *"Commit your works to the Lord, and your thoughts will be established."* Proverbs 16:3.

The *Law of Service* is a simple yet powerful concept that can help us lead a more fulfilling life. It states that we should always aim to serve others as much as possible without expecting anything in return. By doing so, not only do we help others, but we also generate positive energy and attract good things into our lives.

The *Law of Service* is a restorer. Really? Yes, really! We restore ourselves by restoring others freely, with no strings attached. To proactively safeguard ourselves from frivolous temptations, it is best to serve as a restorer, Mentally, Physically, Emotionally, Spiritually, or Financially. Let us align accordingly, *"Brethren, if a man is overtaken in any trespass, you who are spiritual restore such a one in a spirit of gentleness, considering yourself lest you also be tempted. Bear one another's burdens, and so fulfill the law of Christ."* Galatians 6:1-2.

When we serve others, we shift our focus away from ourselves and our own problems. We become more empathetic, compassionate, and understanding, which in turn helps us build stronger relationships with those around us. When we give freely of our time, energy, and resources in the Spirit of Excellence, we create a ripple effect of positivity, touching everyone we encounter.

According to the *Law of Service*, God records our Acts of Service, and even if people refuse to admit our impact, hide us as their best-kept secret, ignore our presence, or downplay our relevance, He will keep multiplying whatever we are giving, sharing, or offering. Really? Yes, really! However, there is a Spiritual Contingency Clause: We must do whatever it is, in the Spirit of Excellence.

Why must we operate in the Spirit of Excellence, especially when we are not perfect? Perfection is a matter of perception, and excellence is a desired heart posture. Here is the pristine mindset of *Service* for the Kingdom: *"Whatever your hand finds to do, do it with your might; for there is no work or device or knowledge or wisdom in the grave where you are going."* Ecclesiastes 9:10. If you are going to do something, do it right or to the best of your ability; if not, kindly opt out!

The *Law of Service* requires us to document our Testament or Testimony. Is this a new requirement for Believers? Absolutely not! It is Ancient! *"Now go, write it before them on a tablet, And note it on a scroll, That it may be for time to come, Forever and ever."* Isaiah 30:8. What if we choose not to document? We have free will to document or not to. Still, it does not change how God feels about us wasting time or living in vain. Blasphemy, right? Wrong. I am not a smooth talker, nor do

I throw the rock and hide my hands. I am going to speak the truth in love, so here is what we must know about this matter: *"That this is a rebellious people, Lying children, Children who will not hear the law of the LORD; Who say to the seers, 'Do not see,' And to the prophets, 'Do not prophesy to us right things; Speak to us smooth things, prophesy deceits. Get out of the way, Turn aside from the path, Cause the Holy One of Israel To cease from before us.' "* Isaiah 30:9-11.

Of course, it is essential to remember that this does not mean we should become martyrs or neglect our own needs. We can still care for ourselves and pursue our goals while serving others. When we do so, we can become even more effective at helping others, operating from a place of strength, clarity, and abundance. As we move into the next phase of service: *"He who has an ear, let him hear what the Spirit says to the churches. To him who overcomes I will give to eat from the tree of life, which is in the midst of the Paradise of God."* Revelation 2:7.

The *Law of Service* is a powerful tool we can all use to improve ourselves, taking us from level to level, in and out of the Kingdom. By embracing this Spiritual Principle as a part of our daily lives, we can create a more just, compassionate, fulfilling, and excelling environment. Here is what the Bible says, *"Do you see a man who excels in his work? He will stand before kings; he will not stand before unknown men."* Proverbs 22:29.

Our Spiritual Gifts, Callings, Talents, Creativity, and Blueprint are not for us. They are for others, benefiting the Kingdom of God. Using them on ourselves means we are not operating at our full potential or are in a Spiritual Deficit. Moreover, we will turn against ourselves and others, similar to Cain, who turned against Abel, his brother.

What do Cain and Abel have to do with the *Law of Service*, our fruits, or potential? Let us revisit this story: In the Book of Genesis 4:1-16, we all know Cain and Abel, the sons of Adam and Eve. Cain was a farmer, while Abel was a shepherd. One day, they both decided to offer sacrifices to God. Abel offered the firstborn of his flock, while Cain offered some of his crops. God accepted Abel's sacrifice but rejected Cain's.

Unfortunately, the rejection made Cain very angry, jealous, rebellious, and problematic. When God questioned Cain about his anger and countenance, giving him time to repent and follow the Spiritual Protocols and Rules set forth, he developed a deaf ear and a stiff neck. God also warned him about the sifting of his mindset before committing a debaucherous act against his brother; still, he ignored Him, taking his brother's life anyway. To add insult to injury, when questioned about his brother's whereabouts, Cain lied and said he did not know. And with loose lips, he told God that he was not his brother's keeper.

Did his loose lips sink his ship? Absolutely. God then cursed Cain and banished him from the land, making him a wanderer. Despite becoming a nomad, God placed a mark on Cain, protecting him from anyone who would try to take his life.

From the first family, this story explains the dangers of envy, jealousy, pride, greed, coveting, competitiveness, and selfishness, and how they can lead to awful consequences while serving God. It also shares the importance of being honest and truthful with God, ourselves, and others. The consequences of whitewashing our mistakes without repenting and changing our thoughts, actions, and reactions can spoil our future fruits.

A Tree will NEVER consume its own fruit; it is for the benefit of others. And whatever is not consumed by others falls to the ground as fertilizer or seeds for the next batch or harvest. We, as Believers, are no different. *"But his delight is in the law of the LORD, And in His law he meditates day and night. He shall be like a tree planted by the rivers of water, That brings forth its fruit in its season, Whose leaf also shall not wither; And whatever he does shall prosper."* Psalm 1:2-3.

What if we consume our own fruits? We will become Mentally, Physically, Emotionally, or Spiritually sick. How so? Envy, jealousy, pride, greed, coveting, competitiveness, hatefulness, anger, and debauchery will consume us with the lust of the eyes, the lust of the flesh, and the pride of life, leading to Spiritual Blindness, Deafness, and Muteness. Is this real? It is as real as the air we breathe. *"The ungodly are not so, But are like the chaff which the wind drives away. Therefore the ungodly shall not stand in the judgment, Nor sinners in the congregation of the righteous. For the LORD knows the way of the righteous, But the way of the ungodly shall perish."* Psalm 1:4-6. Is this not from the Old Testament? Of course. Rebellion and disobedience are the same from the Old Testament to the New Testament, period!

Unfortunately, this is why many Believers who love God walk around with a hole in their hearts, bleeding all over the place, and do not understand why. Sadly, they cannot break yokes, chokeholds, curses, or contend with the enemy's wiles. Meanwhile, we are losing our Kingdom's Credibility among unbelievers.

How is it that no one believes us when we proclaim we are Believers? We are missing the full throttle of the Holy Spirit; as a result, we try too hard to know the Word of God better than the next man but fail to live it, *As It Pleases God*. We fail to serve, *As It Pleases God*. We fail to unveil our Divine Blueprint, *As It Pleases God*. We fail to engage in a *Spirit to Spirit* Relationship, *As It Pleases God*. We fail to document, *As*

It Pleases God. Of course, not all of us, but most of us think God is failing us. But the truth is, we are failing Him.

I get it...no one is perfect, but the Fruits of the Spirit will perfect our character to serve others in Spirit and Truth. When it is all said and done, we must remember, *"God is Spirit, and those who worship Him must worship in Spirit and Truth."* John 4:24.

I have walked this path, and through my Spiritual Journey, I share the Fruits of my Labor. Had I not served broken, tattered, betrayed, and torn, *The WHY Blueprint* or *Build Your Own Table* would not exist. I PROMISE that if we exercise the *Law of Service* with the Fruits of the Spirit, placing the Holy Trinity at the forefront, no one can hold us back from Divine Achievement.

I was given a Promise when I began my Spiritual Journey, knowing nothing, and now here we are. As a Living Testament, the same HAND God extended to me, He also extends to everyone who partakes of this Divine Movement. More importantly, He trusted me as the Messenger to deliver this information, and this *Building Block* will not fail; it will withstand the test of time.

If we do not use the *Law of Service*, we may miss opportunities to connect with others and positively impact the world. Focusing solely on ourselves and our needs may isolate and disconnect us from those around us.

What if we do not like being around people? It is okay if you do not like being around people. The *Law of Service* is not about forcing yourself on anyone; it is about availing yourself to the needs of others. It is about recognizing the value of helping others and finding ways to contribute to society for the greater good, even if it is more introvertedly. There are many ways to serve and make a positive impact, whether through volunteering, donating to causes you care about, or simply being kind and supportive to those around you. You can still live a meaningful life and make a difference, even if you prefer to spend more time alone.

Remember, there is always a way; find it, use it, and grow GREAT.

BUILDING BLOCK 21
Transformation

Are you ready for change? Are you ready to move to the next phase of your Spiritual Journey? Are you resistant to change? Do you fear stepping outside of your comfort zone? Do you lack vision?

We all desire to transform; it is hidden within our DNA. But the question is, 'Are we willing to do the work?' 'Are we willing to be placed into a cocoon?' Unfortunately, this is where most of us give up. It is not that we want to; we just lack the information, understanding, and know-how to stay in the game.

Although some are born into a transformative mindset, some are not. How do I know? I am the first to admit that I was a diamond in the rough. I was not born with a transformative mindset or a silver spoon in my mouth. I was developed, processed, tested, polished, and presented through the *Law of Transformation*.

This Spiritual Law transforms our lives by changing our thoughts, beliefs, words, actions, and reactions. When God places our lives under maintenance, it indicates something greater from within. Most would assume they are under a curse, and others will understand they are Blessed to be a Blessing.

In this phase, the MINDSET determines our Spiritual Status or Levels in the Kingdom. It is not designed to place one person over another; we all have equal rights in the Kingdom, but we will NOT all have equal access to Divine Secrets, Ancient Wisdom, or Heavenly Treasures. Why? First, we must be Spiritually Trained. Secondly, it is for our protection. The higher the level, the higher the consequences are for misuse, misunderstanding, misleading, or misappropriation. Therefore, *"Do not be conformed to this world, but be transformed by the renewing of your mind, that you may prove what is that good and acceptable and perfect will of God."* Romans 12:2.

The best version of ourselves is waiting for us. What if we are at our best? Then my question would be, 'What if we are not?' The Spiritual Tilling process never stops. As long as the seasons change, so do we. The moment we stop, it invokes the Cycle and Vicissitudes of Life to give us a kickstart or place us in a cycle of déjà vu. Why? We are designed to learn, grow, adapt, and sow back into the Kingdom of God.

We may get pruned or cut off when we stop growing, transforming, or using the Fruits of the Spirit. Really? Yes, really! *"Every branch in Me that does not bear fruit He takes away; and every branch that bears fruit He prunes, that it may bear more fruit."* John 15:2.

If our Spiritual Fruits are not producing, transforming, or multiplying, *As It Pleases God*, we experience the sting of unfulfillment, dissatisfaction, disappointment, and frustration. Even if we become excellent at masking it, our psyche tells our story through our habits, words, actions, thoughts, reactions, beliefs, and the lies we tell.

According to our Predestined Blueprint, we can transform our lives and create our desired future with the right mindset and determination. Here are some examples of how the *Law of Transformation* can be applied in or out of the Kingdom, but not limited to such:

- ☐ Define the vision and strategy: Define the vision and strategy for transformation, outlining the desired outcomes, objectives, scope, and timeline.

- ☐ Assess the current state: Assess the current state of the organization, identifying its strengths, weaknesses, opportunities, and threats.

- ☐ Design the future state: Design the future state of the organization, specifying the changes required in its strategy, culture, structure, processes, products, or services.

- ☐ Implement the change: Implement the change plan, allocate resources, assign tasks, execute actions, and manage risks.

- ☐ Monitor and evaluate: Monitor and evaluate the progress and results of transformation, measuring performance indicators, collecting feedback, and making adjustments as needed.

By applying the *Law of Transformation* in these ways, we can create positive change in our lives, achieve our goals and desires, and challenge the norms of our limited ways of thinking.

In the desire to transform, *As It Pleases God*, it is wise to incorporate the *Law of Gratefulness*. Why? In *The WHY Blueprint*, gratefulness is not a stone-alone Spiritual Law; it is also a Spiritual SEAL. We must incorporate it with another one, similar to fueling a fire, gas in a vehicle, or a light bulb in a lamp. *"In everything give thanks; for this is the will of God in Christ Jesus for you."* 1 Thessalonians 5:18.

So, when using the *Law of Gratefulness* as a Spiritual Bonding Agent, the question is, 'What would you like the *Law of Gratefulness* to do for you?' The answer is, 'I want the *Law of Gratefulness* to transform my life, *As It Pleases God*.' What can this do for us?

- ☐ It allows us to comfort each other. *"Therefore comfort each other and edify one another, just as you also are doing."* 1 Thessalonians 5:11.

- ☐ It enables us to recognize others. *"And we urge you, brethren, to recognize those who labor among you, and are over you in the Lord and admonish you."* 1 Thessalonians 5:12.

- ☐ It facilitates being at peace with ourselves and others. *"Esteem them very highly in love for their work's sake. Be at peace among yourselves."* 1 Thessalonians 5:13.

- ☐ It assists us in remaining patient and helpful. *"Now we exhort you, brethren, warn those who are unruly, comfort the fainthearted, uphold the weak, be patient with all."* 1 Thessalonians 5:14.

- ☐ It prevents us from seeking revenge. *"See that no one renders evil for evil to anyone, but always pursue what is good both for yourselves and for all."* 1 Thessalonians 5:15.

- ☐ It helps us rejoice and pray amid all things. *"Rejoice always, pray without ceasing."* 1 Thessalonians 5:16-17.

- ☐ It gives us the ability to test the Spirit. *"Test all things; hold fast what is good."* 1 Thessalonians 5:21.

- ☐ It helps us to back up from evil. *"Abstain from every form of evil."* 1 Thessalonians 5:22.

Can gratefulness revolutionize our lives? Absolutely. Beyond a shadow of a doubt, this happens once we know this one factor: *"Now may the God of peace Himself sanctify you completely; and may your whole spirit, soul, and body be preserved blameless at the coming of our Lord Jesus Christ."* 1 Thessalonians 5:23.

According to our Predestined Blueprint, when we are in Purpose on purpose, here is the rule: *"Be anxious for nothing, but in everything by prayer and supplication, with thanksgiving, let your requests be made known to God."* Philippians 4:6. Once again, GOD first! Why? Once Divine Order is established, *As It Pleases God*, the transformation process will occur naturally. Everything we need is already.

www.DrYBur.com

BUILDING BLOCK 22
Purpose

What is your reason for being? Do you know your purpose? Are you aware of your Gifts, Calling, Talents, Passion, or Creativity? Are you doing what you were called to do? Are you struggling with your identity? Are you maximizing what you have in your hands? These are the questions we face and often do not have the answers to. Yet, the desires are so real that our wishful thinking begins to fabricate lies to satiate our psyche, causing us to whitewash the truth.

In *The WHY Blueprint*, 'What Hurts You is What Heals You,' but more importantly, hurts or traumas often hold your Divine Purpose. If you have not read *The WHY Blueprint*, it is the foundation for *Building Your Own Table*. By transforming your challenges, struggles, pain, rejection, and suffering into opportunities for growth, learning, healing, and service, leaving no stone unturned, you can become a POWERHOUSE for the Kingdom of God.

Our Divine Purpose contains gratitude, faith, or hope to cultivate our purposeful intents, *As It Pleases God.* When we consecrate ourselves to our Predestined Blueprint, the sacrifices, dedications, or devotions become easier. However, if we fight against it, we inadvertently fight against ourselves, taking it out on others.

On the other hand, some get a silver spoon, and others do not. Then again, some feel they are fortunate, lucky, favored, privileged, prosperous, successful, and wealthy in the public eye. Yet, when the stage lights are turned off, it becomes a different story altogether. All in all, in the Eye of God, when it comes to our Divine Purpose or Predestined Blueprint, silver spoon or not, we must Spiritually Till our own ground, putting in the work, *As It Pleases God*. Why? Here again, this is where the *Law of Gratefulness* provides a Spiritual Seal for our *Building Block*.

The goal of this last *Building Block* is to bring our hidden Spiritual Blueprint to the forefront to ensure that when the lights are turned off, we are at peace with ourselves, Mentally, Physically, Emotionally, Spiritually, and Financially. What is the purpose of having peace? Without it, we fall apart while pretending to have it all together.

For me, when someone brags about what they have or do and is clueless about their reason for being…I already know what time it is. What time is it? Deception or distraction time. Why? First, bragging does not move me, nor God. I want to know about their Spiritual Oil or Substance. Secondly, I want to know how a person operates under pressure. Thirdly, I want to hear how someone leverages what comes from their mouth. The bottom line is that I want to know about their people skills. What is the purpose of knowing this information? It tells me who and what I am dealing with based on the Fruits of the Spirit; plus, it reveals what Spiritual Fruits are needed when dealing with them to remain Christlike.

Our reason for being is a creative expression of who we are, and if distractions drown us, we become beguiled by the enemy inside or outside of us. What does this mean? We blame everyone else for not evolving into who we were called to be. For this reason, the *Law of Purpose* calls us out...come out, come out, wherever you are!

Is it possible to call our Divine Purpose forth? Absolutely. If we do not call it forth, who will? It cannot call itself forth. Why? We have free will and were not created as robots; therefore, we must consciously choose to awaken it, Spiritually Tilling our own ground. Here is how, but not limited to such:

- ☐ Start your day with gratitude. Acknowledge and appreciate all the BLESSINGS you already have, such as the breath of life, health, family, friends, work, hobbies, environment, and a roof over your head. Express your gratitude verbally or in writing.

- ☐ Set your intentions for the day. Cluelessness is no longer your portion. You must know the WHAT and WHY of your days.

- ☐ Choose one word, phrase, or Spiritual Fruit representing what you want to focus on or manifest in your day, such as love, joy, peace, kindness, creativity, and so on. Repeat it to yourself throughout the day and act accordingly.

- ☐ If you make a mistake, repent, forgive, self-correct, and keep it moving in the Spirit of Excellence.

- [ ] Be mindful of your thoughts, words, actions, and reactions. Notice how they affect you and others. Are they positive or negative? Are they good or bad? Are they helpful or harmful? Are they aligned with your intentions? If not, change them.

- [ ] Be generous with your time, energy, resources, talents, and gifts. Look for ways to calmly, kindly, or patiently share, serve, and make a difference. Even if you are busy, you do not need to appear impatient, unruly, selfish, or insensitive about your time.

- [ ] Share your skills, knowledge, wisdom, and understanding with others. This wisdom strategy will secretly or openly improve whatever you share for the greater good.

- [ ] Be creative with your challenges, struggles, pains, and sufferings. They all contain underlying or secret wisdom, understandings, or principles to make you better, stronger, and wiser.

- [ ] Learn from your mistakes and failures, document them as a Testament, and share them as a Testimony.

- [ ] Use your experiences to inspire or support others who are going through similar situations.

- [ ] Be joyful with your achievements, failures, successes, and rewards. Celebrate them with yourself and others. Overcoming anything deserves a pat on the back from you.

☐ End your day with reflection. Identify what went well and what can be improved.

If there was a lapse of focus, begin afresh the next day. Every day is new, especially when we are in Purpose on purpose. Know this and use it to your advantage: *"Through the LORD's mercies we are not consumed, Because His compassions fail not. They are new every morning; Great is Your faithfulness."* Lamentations 3:22-23. Using it in our *Spirit to Spirit* Communion time will revolutionize our lives, guaranteed.

According to the Heavenly of Heavens, by dedicating our time, energy, resources, talents, and gifts to a greater good for Kingdom Use, we gain Spiritual Leverage. What does this mean? We have more leverage with God than someone who ignores Him, spends their energy engaging in folly, uses their resources recklessly, buries their talents, or buys love from those who do not give a rat's tail about them.

Using the Fruits of the Spirit is always best when dealing with the *Law of Purpose*. Why? It cuts down on the negative energy we absorb from tomfoolery. When in Purpose on purpose, the Blood of Jesus covers us, and the Holy Spirit guides us. We do not want them to lie dormant due to the lack of self-control or debauchery; thus, we must protect them and operate in the Spirit of Righteousness to the best of our ability.

Is the Blood of Jesus not a one-and-done event? Yes and no. Yes, the Blood has been shed on the cross as Atonement for our sins. However, repentance must occur, and then we must willfully apply the Blood over ourselves, the situation, circumstance, event, or whatever. If no other sins occur in this particular matter, and change has occurred, then the Blood of Jesus will suffice.

On the other hand, if there is a recurring sin, additional sins, habits, negativity, or debauchery, the answer is 'no,' it is not a one-and-done occurrence. We need to repent and reapply the Blood to whatever, with whomever. We do not want to become lax; the enemy awaits us to slip up. For this reason, being that we are not perfect, we should continually repent, cover ourselves, and anoint the doorpost of our homes with the Blood of Jesus, ushering in the Holy Spirit. It is FREE; it costs us nothing, but one slip in the wrong direction can cost us everything.

What if we do not believe in the Blood of Jesus? We have free will to believe whatever we desire, but it does not negate the potency of the BLOOD! We choose our hard...there will always be an option to cover or uncover ourselves. What does this mean? A sacrifice will be made regardless of what we believe. In the Kingdom of God, the Blood of Jesus is our Sacrifice of Atonement. Whereas on the dark side, anything goes. Really? Yes, really! Once again, we choose our hard!

To unveil our Divine Blueprint, we must be covered by the Blood of Jesus; if not, we cannot obtain the whole portion of our Blueprinted Purpose. Why? It is Spiritually Guarded, similar to the Garden of Eden in the Book of Genesis.

What if we have it going on and are operating in our purpose without this Jesus stuff? Congratulations. Nevertheless, having it going on in the Eye of God is a matter of perception. Why? Self-created purpose differs from our Divine Purpose. One creates a yoke, and the other breaks yokes. Having what money can buy is different from having what money cannot. The goal is to have BOTH. According to the Heavenly of Heavens, to do so, *As It Pleases Him*, there must be Divine Order.

Once we gain Spiritual Access and understand our Divine Purpose, *As It Pleases God,* we want to protect it, especially when having what money cannot buy. Why? We can set goals, achieve them, and make decisions that align with them instead of plugging and playing on the wrong path, leading us into the PIT. Remember that everyone has their own unique Spiritual Journey, and it is okay to diverge from the paths of others. When dealing with our Divine Blueprint, there is no reason to fret, fuss, or fight; what is for us will be, and what is not cannot remain.

What if we are unsure? It is entirely normal to feel unsure of our Divine Purpose at times. To be sure, we will journey through uncertainty from time to time; this is what faith, trust, belief, and hope are all about. It took me many years to figure it out, yet my documentation, *As It Pleased God,* became the Spiritual Lamp illuminating the way. What does this mean? I did not leave it to chance, nor did I leave it to memory. If I did, I would have perished. For this reason, I do not pull any punches regarding documenting, especially when dealing with our Divine Blueprint.

What if we have a good memory? Congratulations. Geniuses are not recognized by what they remember; they are revered by what they document and leave behind for the next man. What if we are not geniuses? We are all geniuses to our Divine Mission or reason for being; we have simply forgotten. With all due respect, if we think our memory makes us smart, we are utterly deceived. Why? If what we know, understand, and glean from life stops with us, I must shake my head in dismay. We are Blessed to be a Blessing, and our Predestined Blueprint is designed to enlighten the path for others.

Connecting with our Divine Purpose can be a challenging but fulfilling process. It requires self-reflection and exploration of our interests and values. Here are some steps you can take to help you connect with your Divine Purpose, but not limited to such:

- ☐ Reflect on your values: Take some time to consider what is important to you. What values guide your life? What do you stand for? What will you not accept?
- ☐ Explore your interests: Try new things and see what resonates with you. What activities bring you joy and fulfillment?
- ☐ Seek guidance: Do not be afraid to contact trusted friends, family members, or professionals for support and guidance. They may have insights that can help you on your journey.
- ☐ Embrace the journey: Remember that your purpose may evolve and change over time. Stay open to new possibilities and enjoy the process of discovering your Divine Purpose.
- ☐ Assess your strengths and weaknesses.
- ☐ Reflect on your past experiences.
- ☐ Document what you have learned from them.
- ☐ Think about what you would do if you had unlimited resources.
- ☐ Consider what you would do if you were not afraid of failure.
- ☐ Brainstorm a list of potential interests, ideas, desires, or passions.
- ☐ Take personality and career assessments to gain more insight.
- ☐ Volunteer or intern in the areas of interest to gain experience.

- ☐ Attend conferences, workshops, seminars, outings, or meetings related to your interests.
- ☐ Read books or articles on topics that inspire you.
- ☐ Consider how you can positively impact the world.
- ☐ Set goals and create a plan to achieve them.
- ☐ Surround yourself with supportive people who encourage and challenge you.
- ☐ Reflect regularly on your progress and make adjustments as needed.

Suppose your purpose feels like a burden. Taking a step back and re-evaluating what it means to you is ideal. When straddling the fence in this matter, your purpose should bring meaning and fulfillment to your life, not add unnecessary stress. All this means is that misalignment is somewhere; this is how we go from regular purpose to Divine Purpose. Nevertheless, when faced with this ordeal, the first place to look is in the area of our passion.

Divine Status

Passion and purpose can differ, and they can war against each other. Why would war take place? They are designed to complement each other for the greater good. When finding your purpose, it is essential to consider how it aligns with your passions. Your purpose should bring meaning and fulfillment to your life, and if it does not align with your passions, it may feel like a burden, which means it is not DIVINE yet. Take some time to evaluate whether your current purpose aligns with your passions, and if not, consider making changes to bring more alignment and fulfillment, *As It Pleases God.*

How can we take our passion and purpose to a Divine Status? Our Divine Status, *As It Pleases God*, is hidden within our WHY. If it is all about us, it may not be Divine at its present state because our mindset is not yet aligned with the Heavenly of Heavens, limiting our Kingdom Usability. Simply put, if our passion and purpose only benefit our family or us, and that is it, and not for the greater good of the Kingdom of God, more than likely, it is not at a Divine Status.

No judgment intended; I am only the Messenger. Please allow me to break this down: Our passion and purpose are often intertwined, but it is essential to understand the difference between the two to get to the Divine Status. Passion is something we love and enjoy doing, while purpose is WHY we do it. Meanwhile, our Divine Status is WHO we do it for. If we DO NOT add God into our equational efforts, *As It Pleases Him*, our passion or purpose remains at a lower level with Spiritual Limits, even if we have serious cash flow.

How do we make passion and purpose make sense? Dealing with our Divine Status is not limited to a pulpit, the pews, knocking on doors, or passing out pamphlets. According to the Heavenly of Heavens, it is more about using what we have in our hands (Gifts, Calling, Talents, Creativity, Passion, and Skills). For example, if our passion is music, our purpose could be to use our music to inspire and uplift the downtrodden.

Another example could be if our passion is cooking; our purpose could be to use our culinary skills to help others by volunteering at a soup kitchen or starting a food blog to share recipes and cooking tips. Finding the right balance between our passion and purpose can lead to a fulfilling and meaningful life, and by adding the Holy Trinity (The Father,

Son, and Holy Spirit) and the Fruits of the Spirit into the equation, *As It Pleases Him*, we can take whatever we are doing into a Divine Status.

When dealing with our Divine Status, there is nothing magical or spooky about it; it is our reality. Everyone has this potential, but not everyone uses it. *The WHY Blueprint* and *Build Your Own Table* are designed to eliminate the kinks in this area; however, when doing so, it is entirely okay to adjust and evolve in your Divine Purpose and Passion over time.

Here is the deal: I did not come straight out of the gate as a writer. I began with a letter, and fortunately, that letter continued into multiple books, seminars, workshops, videos, and so on. My PASSION is to help others, and my Divine Purpose is to WRITE, documenting the WAY, according to my Predestined Blueprint. But if we back up for a moment, my goal was to become an Attorney at Law when I DID NOT understand my Divine Purpose. After getting my Divine Blueprint laid out *Spirit to Spirit* with an understanding, *As It Pleased God*, I transitioned to my rightful position as a Spiritual Doctor, Lawyer, and Oracle for a time such as this.

My Spiritual Training from the Heavenly of Heavens was not a joke, nor do I wish it upon anyone; therefore, I provide proven and guaranteed road maps, mind maps, and results from the inside out. Amid my Spiritual Training, Testing, and Remedial stages, I was mocked, ridiculed, and thrown under the bus as if it were a game. But God, as the Spiritual Tables turned, *Building My Own Table*, they are not laughing now. Therefore, do not despise the day of small beginnings; follow *The WHY Blueprint*, and no one or nothing can stop your Divine Destiny, especially when activating the *Law of Reciprocity*.

Reciprocity

The *Law of Reciprocity* is a Spiritual Principle of giving and receiving and a version of the *Law of Seedtime and Harvest*. What is the difference? The Mindset of Multiplicity. Our Divine Status comes with multiplying factors, and if we GIVE BACK to the Kingdom of God, we will receive more. Not more in selfishness, but based on our Divine Well or Underlying Cistern designed as Provision for the Vision. What does this mean? Whatever is needed for our Predestined Blueprint is already there, and the *Law of Reciprocity* helps us tap into it or cause it to overflow.

When someone does something nice for you, it is easy to feel grateful and appreciative. In addition, it is also important to remember that gratitude alone may not be enough. You need to take action and show your appreciation tangibly. Picturesquely, this gesture could be as simple as sending a thank-you note or as elaborate as taking someone out for dinner. Why must we be grateful and appreciative? It is in our nature to be on the take, abuse, or compete against our conveyance system.

Do we not possess a competitive nature? Absolutely! Competing against man is one thing, but secretly competing against God Almighty is another. For this reason, we must tame the underlying beast. Ungratefulness clogs our Divine Cistern, causing the *Law of Reciprocity* to backfire due to feelings of entitlement. The same way we treat others indicates how we treat God, our Heavenly Father. Blasphemy, right? Wrong. John 14:15 states, *"If you love Me, keep My commandments."*

The *Law of Reciprocity* is not just about repaying kindness; it is also about initiating it. By being the first to extend kindness to others, you set a positive example and create a ripple effect of generosity and goodwill. So the next time you have the opportunity to do something kind for someone else, seize it. You never know how much of an impact it might have.

Giving and receiving are critical for building and maintaining a healthy relationship with God, yourself, and others, fostering trust, and creating a sense of connection. When you give to others, you show them that you care and are willing to invest in them. If someone says you have no value to them, believe them without trying to convince them, politely excuse yourself, and keep it moving in the Spirit of Excellence.

Meanwhile, receiving is essential because it allows others to show their care, concern, value, and appreciation for you, but you must release the expectations associated. It would be best for the human psyche if you DO NOT make someone do something they choose not to do. Why? Most traumas, hurts, pains, or disappointments are derived from false, broken, or violated expectations.

Here is the ideal mindset, *As It Pleases God*: If someone wants to give, they will. If they do not, they will not. Violating the free will of another, who is not your child to train in the Ways of God, or forcing them to do something out of selfishness and not righteousness, creates a Spiritual Violation with a negative backlash. Even God does not force us to love Him, but He has the power to do so and does not violate our free will.

For example, babies are not born sharing automatically; they are selfish by default, needing to be taught to share with others and not take what does not belong to them. Some parents go overboard, teaching their children not to beg, give, or receive. And some opt for or implant the get-all-you-can-get hustle mentality. Either way, and *As It Pleases God*, we must learn and understand what He expects from us, especially regarding *The WHY Blueprint* and how to *Build Our Own Tables* properly with what is DIVINE.

One way to make the *Law of Reciprocity* work for us is to be mindful of our actions, thoughts, words, and intentions. When we do something for someone else, it should come from a genuine desire to help, rather than as a means to get something in return. Additionally, we should be open to receiving help from others when we need it, without expecting anything in return. We can create positive and mutually beneficial relationships with those around us by approaching the *Law of Reciprocity* with this mindset.

When initiating the *Law of Reciprocity*, we must become intentional at first to develop our skill of paying attention. What is the purpose of becoming intentional? It makes us proactive, Kingdomly Proactive, to be exact.

The WHY Blueprint (What Hurts You is What Heals You) is also designed to pinpoint What Heals Others. Therefore, we must develop our Mind-Eye, Hand-Eye, and Heart-Eye Coordination, knowing when to move, give, receive, or reject. Can we really master this ability? Absolutely. Listed below are a few ways to begin developing the *Law of Reciprocity*, Ironclad Mentality (Iron sharpens Iron), but not limited to such:

- ☐ Offer to help someone in need without expecting anything in return.
- ☐ Pay for someone's meal or coffee without them knowing.
- ☐ Volunteer your time at a local charity or non-profit organization.

- ☐ Give a compliment to someone you appreciate or admire.
- ☐ Listen actively and be present when someone needs to talk.
- ☐ Share your expertise or skills with someone who could benefit from them.
- ☐ Send a thoughtful note or message to someone you care about.
- ☐ Offer to babysit or pet-sit for a friend or neighbor.
- ☐ Offer to run errands for someone unable to do so themselves.
- ☐ Share a helpful resource or article with someone who could use the information.
- ☐ Offer to cook or bring food for someone who is going through a tough time.
- ☐ Offer to help someone move or pack if they are moving.
- ☐ Give a gift or send flowers to someone to brighten their day.
- ☐ Share your knowledge or experience with someone who is just starting out.
- ☐ Offer to help a colleague with a project or task.
- ☐ Be a mentor or coach to someone who could benefit from your guidance.
- ☐ Offer to be a sounding board or confidant to someone who needs to talk.
- ☐ Give someone a ride or offer to carpool to save on gas.
- ☐ Offer to do someone's laundry or help with household chores if they have limited mobility.
- ☐ Accept help from others when you need it, recognizing that we all need support occasionally.

Sharing is a fundamental aspect of the *Building Block* mentality. Why? *"As iron sharpens iron, so a man sharpens the countenance of his friend."* Proverbs 27:17. Besides, our Divine Purpose is all about building each other positively for Kingdom Usage.

What if we are rejected when using the *Law of Reciprocity*? First and foremost, it builds Kingdom Durability, ensuring we do not fall apart Mentally, Physically, Emotionally, or Spiritually when rejected. According to the Heavenly of Heavens, rejection is one of the Spiritual Classrooms we do not want to fail. Why should we not fail the Class of Rejection? Our Divine Purpose requires the lessons to become more challenging with each remedial course. Thus putting us on a cycle of déjà vu until we pass or learn how to withstand the Winds, Storms, Rains, Coldness, and Sunlight of Rejection.

Secondly, it is understandable to feel anxious about the possibility of rejection when sharing something personal with someone. However, it is essential to remember that how someone reacts to our vulnerability says more about them than it does about us. If someone rejects us for sharing, it may be because they are uncomfortable with vulnerability or have their own issues to work through. As long as we learn what we need to learn, glean what we need to glean, understand what we need to understand, and do what needs to be done, *As It Pleases God*, the deal is SEALED in the Kingdom. So, do not worry about it; keep it moving in the Spirit of Excellence.

Thirdly, our worth and value as a person are not determined by the reactions, thoughts, words, or beliefs of others. Our OBEDIENCE and SELF-DISCIPLINE will determine our Divine Worth and Value in the Eye of God

Almighty. By using *The WHY Blueprint* and *Building Your Own Table* in such a manner, and *As It Pleases God*, we can build deeper connections and create opportunities for growth and healing for ourselves and others with no shame attached.

Self-Discipline

The *Law of Self-Discipline* is a POWERFUL Spiritual Tool that helps us stay on the right track, controlling our impulses to make better decisions, especially when embarking upon our Divine Purpose with our Predestined Blueprint.

Most use the *Law of Self-Discipline* as a standalone. But for *The Why Blueprint* and *Building Your Own Table*, the *Law of Purpose* includes the *Law of Self-Discipline*. Why? Discipline is a prerequisite for receiving *Spirit to Spirit* downloaded instructions for our Divine Blueprint. Although perfection is not required, discipline is. Why? In the Eye of God, the lack of discipline, disobedience, dullness, pompousness, and stiff necks are sore spots for God, bringing wrath and laxness.

According to the Heavenly of Heavens, the do-nothing mentality will not get it. We have been twiddling our thumbs and being deceived for too long. Once again, we must Spiritually Till our own ground, doing what it takes to Spiritually Align ourselves, *As It Pleases God*. While simultaneously saying 'no' to unrighteousness and 'yes' to what is right, just, good, and fair.

The WHY Blueprint is about setting clear goals, creating a plan of action, and sticking to it no matter what. It also means saying 'no' to things that might distract you. With self-discipline, you can overcome any obstacle and achieve anything you want that aligns with your Predestined

Blueprint. Listed below are a few ways to develop self-discipline, but not limited to such:

- ☐ Set clear goals and priorities for yourself.
- ☐ Create a daily routine and stick to it.
- ☐ Use a planner for notes, thoughts, or ideas.
- ☐ Use a calendar to schedule your tasks.
- ☐ Take breaks and rest when needed, but do not let them become distractions.
- ☐ Avoid procrastination by starting a task as soon as possible.
- ☐ Break down complex tasks into smaller, more manageable ones.
- ☐ Reward yourself for achieving milestones.
- ☐ Surround yourself with positive and motivated people.
- ☐ Avoid negative influences, distractions, or foolery.
- ☐ Visualize success and the benefits of discipline.
- ☐ Stay focused on the task at hand and avoid multitasking until you become a pro.
- ☐ Monitor your progress and adjust your strategies as needed.
- ☐ Stay accountable by sharing your goals with others.
- ☐ Create a support system or find a mentor.
- ☐ Stay healthy and take care of your physical and mental well-being.
- ☐ Learn from your mistakes, and do not let them discourage you.
- ☐ Stay motivated by reminding yourself of your Divine Purpose and why you started.
- ☐ Stay organized and tidy as much as possible to reduce distractions and stress.

☐ Stay consistent and persistent in your efforts toward achieving your goals.

Developing a positive mental mindset with self-discipline is one of the most important things you can do for yourself. With practice, you can train your mind to stay optimistic and motivated, even in difficult times. Remember, developing a positive, ironclad mental mindset with self-discipline is a journey of self-improvement, not a destination.

Self-Improvement

Self-improvement is essential to personal growth and development, and Spiritual Autonomy, *As It Pleases God*. Without it, Spiritual Autonomy is not granted. Why? We cannot handle it. Says who? Says the one who refuses to learn, grow, and sow back into the Kingdom of God. The process of making conscious efforts to enhance one's skills, knowledge, and abilities to achieve personal and professional goals is on us, not God.

Furthermore, if we cannot improve with earthly laws and principles, we cannot contend with Spiritual Principles, Laws, and Protocols. Nor should we try...attempting to outdo God is a big no-no.

The *Law of Self-Improvement* wants us to know that every individual has the potential to become better and succeed in life if they continuously work on themselves. Hence, we must take responsibility for growth and development and commit to lifelong learning, growing, and developing. If we do not do this for anyone else, we should do this for ourselves.

Refusing to grow or improve ourselves can cause us to become a negative cesspool, stagnant thinkers, unfulfilled, short-sighted, or insecure. No offense intended! God wants to bring us out from among the negative clouds of deceit. Is this Biblical? Absolutely. *"The harp and the strings, The tambourine and flute, And wine are in their feasts; But they do not regard the work of the LORD, Nor consider the operation of His hands. Therefore my people have gone into captivity, Because they have no knowledge; Their honorable men are famished, And their multitude dried up with thirst. Therefore Sheol has enlarged itself And opened its mouth beyond measure; Their glory and their multitude and their pomp, And he who is jubilant, shall descend into it. People shall be brought down, Each man shall be humbled, And the eyes of the lofty shall be humbled."* Isaiah 5:12-15.

Even as Believers, we cannot stop growing in Spiritual Wisdom, Astuteness, and Proactiveness. What if we are a Spiritual Elite who knows everything about the Bible? Knowing everything does not mean we understand the Mind of God, nor does it grant us Divine Access to Spiritual Wisdom, Secrets, or Treasures; therefore, we can never lower our Spiritual Antennas. The moment we do, we will 'get got' by the enemy's wiles.

When we think we have arrived Mentally, Physically, Emotionally, Spiritually, or Financially in the Realm of the Spirit, it means we are at a dead-end. Why? We must stay on READY, on a learning curve, and ten toes deep in the Kingdom, using the Fruits of the Spirit and behaving Christlike to avoid Spiritual Woes.

Anything or anyone, DIVINE or not, must grow; lacking it means a woe-able death. What does this mean? Please allow me to approach this sensitive topic with four Biblical Woes:

- ☐ *"Woe to those who draw iniquity with cords of vanity, And sin as if with a cart rope, That say, 'Let Him make speed and hasten His work, That we may see it; And let the counsel of the Holy One of Israel draw near and come, That we may know it.' "* Isaiah 5:18-19.

- ☐ *"Woe to those who call evil good, and good evil; Who put darkness for light, and light for darkness; Who put bitter for sweet, and sweet for bitter!"* Isaiah 5:20.

- ☐ *"Woe to those who are wise in their own eyes, And prudent in their own sight!"* Isaiah 5:21.

- ☐ *"Woe to men mighty at drinking wine, Woe to men valiant for mixing intoxicating drink, Who justify the wicked for a bribe, And take away justice from the righteous man!"* Isaiah 5:22-23.

Finally, let us sum this up: *"Therefore, as the fire devours the stubble, And the flame consumes the chaff, So their root will be as rottenness, And their blossom will ascend like dust; Because they have rejected the law of the LORD of hosts, And despised the word of the Holy One of Israel."* Isaiah 5:24.

Regarding personal growth, *As It Pleases God*, daily self-improvement is the key to success, while narcissism can hinder it. Here are a few ways to help us become the best version of ourselves, but not limited to such:

- ☐ Set goals and work towards them.
- ☐ Practice gratitude daily.

- ☐ Learn from mistakes and failures.
- ☐ Cultivate self-awareness.
- ☐ Build positive relationships.
- ☐ Prioritize self-care and rest.
- ☐ Develop healthy habits.
- ☐ Read and educate oneself.
- ☐ Embrace change and adapt quickly without complaining.
- ☐ Make time for reflection and meditation.
- ☐ Practice empathy and compassion.
- ☐ Seek feedback and guidance from trusted sources.
- ☐ Step out of your comfort zone and take risks.
- ☐ Practice effective communication.
- ☐ Be accountable for your actions and decisions.
- ☐ Use the Fruits of the Spirit without wavering.
- ☐ Volunteer and give back to the community.
- ☐ Practice forgiveness and let go of grudges.
- ☐ Stay open-minded and curious.
- ☐ Celebrate successes and acknowledge the progress made.

Our thoughts, actions, reactions, words, and beliefs are powerful, and we must be mindful of the energy we are exuding or absorbing. I have found that one of the best ways to cultivate a positive mindset is by practicing gratitude.

According to *The WHY Blueprint*, when honing in on our Predestined Blueprint, we must focus on what money CANNOT buy. This reflective practice of gratefulness causes us to pay attention to the small things that profoundly impact us.

I have been where you are, and I do not take this Spiritual Journey or *The WHY Blueprint* for granted. When everyone walked away from me, and I mean EVERYONE, no one was spared. I had to continue to move forward, focusing on my *Spirit to Spirit* Connection with my Heavenly Father, regardless of how it appeared.

Irrespective of who stayed or left, threw me under the bus, refused to help me, dragged my name through the dirt, lied about me, or pilfered my business ideas and spat in my face, I had to keep a smile on my face with my head held high. More importantly, I had to move forward in the Spirit of Excellence and Kindness, *Building My Own Table*, and doing what I am Divinely Called to do. And now, here we are!

I never thought that asking for help from those I have helped, inspired, motivated, and protected without fail would be a problem for them. Those I helped considered me asking for help with simple things, having nothing to do with money, fame, or fortune, as begging. On this Spiritual Journey, I never thought I would see such bigotry from individuals who continue to glean wisdom from me to better their lives and pad their pockets.

You see, I am NOT speaking of the average, nothing to offer, Joe Blow. I am speaking of the well-known, well-to-do millionaires who gained more from my suffering than from offering me a helping hand. Yet, they consciously chose to hide me as their best-kept secret, as if God wanted me to play small, remain hidden, as if my boat capsized, my sail would not bring me to the shore, or no one would ever know about their secret TRAIL of Wisdom. But God said, 'NOT SO!'

Although I had to build from the ground up, block by block, God was faithful. I continually engaged in self-improvement with Him at the forefront, doing what most can only dream about doing with their bare hands. I am a

Living Testimony of how to *Build Your Own Table*, allowing my WHY to become the Divine Blueprint, leading the next man into their GREATNESS.

According to my FOREFATHERS, and the Promise from the Ancient of Days until now, EVERYONE has the right to glean from the same hidden TRAIL of Wisdom, leaving no willing man behind. For this reason, when a man is down, we should never kick them, especially when they are Manifesting and Co-Creating, *As It Pleases God*. What is so special about Manifesting and Co-Creating, *As It Pleases God*? Because their COMEBACK could make us hang our heads down in shame.

But for me, I want the STORY! Why? It is the TESTIMONY of my comeback, *As It Pleases God*, that sets the record straight. They, meaning many people, thought God had abandoned me, trying to convince me of this falsity to justify their absence. Meanwhile, they called me names and negatively labeled me to justify their atrocious behaviors. To add insult to injury, some even tried to inadvertently cause me to doubt God's Promises. How? By trying to outright manipulate me into giving up, convince me to hide under a rock, hang my head down in shame, or build their dreams in exchange for forgetting about mine. Really? Yes, really!

After making many mistakes, bad decisions, and falling for the okey-doke, I knew better than to step outside of God's Divine Will. Willful disobedience got me into this situation, and it would take Divine Obedience to get me out; therefore, if it was not Spiritually Aligning with my Predestined Blueprint, *As It Pleased God*, it or they had to exit. God was TRAINING me, and I had to stay focused.

Most would ask, 'How could I hold on after being abandoned, put six feet under while still alive, and still operate in my right frame of mind?' First, I did not flinch an inch because I had my Spiritual Journey DOCUMENTED, and everything began to ALIGN accordingly. And those who were trying to manipulate me could not hit a lick at a crooked stick, had nothing documented, and were clueless about their reason for being.

Secondly, God was audibly speaking and instructing me, step-by-step, as I was doing what most people cannot. If God was downloading the Divine Information within me, it meant He had not left me—so I was not alone or lonely. Therefore, while they were busy having fun, laughing, and intentionally excluding me, I was busy *Building My Own Table* and placing a Spiritual Seal on *The Why Blueprint* (What Hurts You is What Heals You).

Thirdly, if I was manifesting, *As It Pleased God*, developing the Divine Discipline needed to get guaranteed results, I was on to something BIG. I was unwilling to throw all of my work down the drain because someone did not agree with God's Divine Method of Spiritual Training for my Predestined Blueprint. Here is what I know: *"God has chosen the foolish things of the world to put to shame the wise, and God has chosen the weak things of the world to put to shame the things which are mighty."* 1 Corinthians 1:27.

Lastly, He was delivering me from people and their opinions that were designed to misalign or distract me from my Predestined Blueprint. If they could not hear what I heard, see what I have seen, speak my language, or correctly confirm who sent them, they did not stand a chance at aborting the Mission of God. As a result, I learn what I need to learn with an understanding, and I keep it moving in the Spirit of Excellence without batting an eye.

All in all, my experiences cleared my Spiritual Eyes, Ears, and Voice, allowing me to vibrate at a higher frequency. Really? Yes. Really! With a Manifesting Power, putting to boot the concealment for the Divine Unveiling of *The WHY Blueprint* and the *As It Pleases God* Movement.

In a nutshell, they tried their best, but God was more brilliant, much better, wiser, and more strategic, allowing my enemies to become my footstool! What does this mean? God used my enemies as a propellant. They thought they were doing something big by intentionally oppressing, sabotaging, obstructing, or using my weaknesses against me. Meanwhile, God used all of it to position me securely in my Divine Mission.

After all of this, and a little bit of that, do you think for a minute that those who walked away tried to return? Do you think they regretted serving me walking papers or leaving me out? Of course. Even though they thought it would have cost them too much to join my Spiritual Journey, all I have to say is, 'THANK YOU.'

Why would I thank them? I thanked them for unjustly walking away to choose better for themselves. I thanked them for the LESSONS and the TRAINING that I needed to break out of my little cocoon. I thanked them for the opportunity to allow me to move on. I thanked them for allowing me to turn my stepping stones into Divine Cornerstones of Greatness for the Kingdom and to feed God's sheep with tried and tested experiences. More importantly, I thanked them for taking their walking shoes on their way out, which allowed me to shake the dust off my feet with zero regrets and zero residual baggage. All of which allowed me to MASTER my ability to use the Fruits of the Spirit and behave Christlike, earning my Spiritual Stripes, *As It Pleased God*. So, you see, I bear no grudges...only

GRATEFULNESS because I left them better off than when I met them, setting the Spiritual Benchmark of authenticity and integrity.

As the dust has settled, I formally present the Spiritual Laws on how to *Build Your Own Table*. By staying committed, persistent, and open-minded, you can achieve your dreams and live the life you have always wanted. Your Predestined Blueprint is now at your beck and call. As you call it forth, *As It Pleases God*, the process may not always be easy, but the rewards will be worth it in the end; I am living proof. Grow GREAT!

Dr. Y. Bur

www.ingramcontent.com/pod-product-compliance
Lightning Source LLC
Chambersburg PA
CBHW071434160426
43195CB00013B/1902